Currier's Quick and Easy Guide to

SALTWATER ƒLY FISHING

Currier's Quick and Easy Guide to

SALTWATER

*f*LY FISHING

by Jeff Currier

WITH ILLUSTRATIONS AND PHOTOGRAPHS BY Jeff Currier
AND FLY PHOTOGRAPHS BY Doug O'looney
FOREWORD BY Paul Bruun

Greycliff Publishing Company
Helena, Montana

PRINTED IN THE UNITED STATES OF AMERICA.

For information, address Greycliff Publishing Company, P.O. Box 1273, Helena, MT 59624.

TYPESET IN MONOTYPE BODONI AND MYRIAD ROMAN BY
Arrow Graphics, Missoula, Montana

COVER DESIGN BY Geoff Wyatt, Helena, Montana

PRINTED BY Advanced Litho Printing, Great Falls, Montana

10 09 08 07 06 05 04 03 02 01 00 99   10 9 8 7 6 5 4 3 2 1

LIBRARY OF CONGRESS CATALOGING-IN-PUBLICATION DATA

Currier, Jeff, 1965–
      Currier's quick and easy guide to saltwater fly fishing / by Jeff Currier ;
with illustrations and photographs by Jeff Currier and fly photographs by
Doug O'looney ; foreword by Paul Bruun.
            p.   cm.
      Includes bibliographical references and index.
      ISBN 0-9626663-9-4 (alk. paper)
      1. Saltwater fly fishing.   I. Title.
SH456.2.C88   1998
799'.16-dc21
                                                            97-42075
                                                               CIP

Dedicated to Dad—longtime fishing partner and friend.

CONTENTS

ILLUSTRATIONS

ACKNOWLEDGMENTS

THIS BOOK WOULD NOT HAVE BEEN POSSIBLE without the hours of assistance and moral support from my father Charles and my wife Yvonne, as well as the rest of my family who constantly support what I do. Dad, an avid fly fisherman himself, started me fishing at age three, creating the monster that I am now. After thirty years of working hard to raise his family rather than going fishing, I have since gotten him back into the sport and even introduced him to saltwater fly fishing.

I am fortunate to have fished many hours in the salt with close friend Paul Bruun, who has a lifetime of experience fly fishing the ocean. Paul, a well-known guide of Wyoming and Idaho, writer, and member of the Orvis Saltwater Advisory Staff, is the most knowledgeable angler that I have ever met. He gladly gave me help and advice whenever I needed it, and generously took hours of his own time to thoroughly read through my early book drafts. I am very thankful for the input and expertise that he has provided, and am proud that he has written the foreword.

I would like to thank my employer, Jack Dennis, author of three very popular fly tying manuals, producer of many fine instructional fly tying and fly fishing videos, and owner of the Jack Dennis Outdoor Shop. It was his example that sparked my initiative to write a book in the first place. I have always appreciated the fact that he has not been just a typical "boss," but rather one of my best friends for many years.

My immediate boss, Larry Bashford, general manager of the Jack Dennis Outdoor Shop, also needs to be credited for allowing me the time to explore the salt. Few bosses would let any employee take off as much time as I have over the years. Although he often may not approve of my frequent trips, he has yet to force cancellation of any of them. He obviously knows how much I truly love this sport.

My first serious trips to the salt are what really got me going. They would not have been possible if it were not for the owners of Belize River

Lodge, Mike and Marguerite Heusner, and Turneffe Flats Lodge owner Craig Hayes, who allowed me to visit their wonderful lodges and fish the waters of Belize many years ago. Then there are my two friends from Key Largo, Florida, Jack Legier and Bob Berman, who showed me around the Florida Keys and parts of the Everglades. Jimmy Nix, well-known for his expertise in tying bass and saltwater flies and for an immense amount of knowledge of saltwater fly fishing, teased many Pacific sailfish and one blue marlin to within my fly casting range in Costa Rica, triggering my interest in blue water fly fishing. Mike Fitzgerald Jr., Bill Goehring, and Jo Ann Poffel of Frontiers International, who together have fished most of the premiere saltwater destinations throughout the world, have also been a big help, always loading me up with the necessary information about saltwater destinations that I choose to visit.

Although I have learned a great deal about fly fishing the salt on my own, I have had invaluable instruction from friends and guides. One of my best friends, Gary Willmott, has accompanied me on more fishing trips than any other person. Together we have survived horrendous blizzards while jigging frozen lakes for lake trout and been blown off the best waters in the West in his first and last high-sided drift boat. He once enticed me to visit him in the Cayman Islands, where I finally landed my first two permit on a fly by taking his advice on when to visit, and by using the fly he recommended.

Scott Sanchez deserves a special thanks. Scott is by far one of the most creative and innovative fly tiers that I have ever known. We worked together for eight years in the Jack Dennis Outdoor Shop, and rarely did a day pass when I did not witness something new from his vise. Whether it's the duct tape squid or the body fur bait fish, Scott always makes sure that for every trip I go on, my fly boxes are full of some of his exciting new patterns.

Ten years ago, the only memories of my fishing trips were recorded on point-and-shoot cameras. Since then I have been extremely fortunate to fish with Tom Montgomery and Andy Anderson, two good friends, fly fishermen, and probably the finest of fly fishing photographers. Much of each of their work consistently appears in the popular fly fishing and various outdoor magazines. Every time I fish with one of them, gobs of camera gear follows. Today, thanks to their willingness to always share their expertise, my own photography skills have been sharpened enough to help with this book.

Skip Gibson and Mike Atwell, who, between the two of them, represent some of the finest fly fishing tackle in the industry, have always helped to outfit me with affordable tackle from fly rods and reels to tippets and flies. Kevin Thompson, of the Sage Rod Company, is always eager to loan me rods and reels as well as Steve Pogano, of Scott Rods, who even let my destruction of one of their custom 14-weight fly rods slide without penalty. Tom McCullough and Marty Downy of the Cortland Line Company have always made sure my fly reels were full with the latest and greatest of saltwater fly lines.

Will Beard, a past fellow Jack Dennis Outdoor Shop employee, critiqued and tested all my knot drawings, which were the most difficult part of creating this book. The other Jack Dennis Outdoor Shop employees, especially the fishing department, always kept the quality control up on all of my art work and photographs used throughout the book. Friends such as Derek Mitchell, Sam Vigneri, Adam Cohen, John Jazwa, Mark Rieser, Mike Kenfield, and Paul Doty, joined me on some of the most thrilling saltwater experiences of my life.

Lastly, I thank Stan Bradshaw for his many hours of time seeing through the publication of this book. He not only carefully read and edited this book several times, but also tested the thoroughness of my information on his first saltwater fly fishing trip. I greatly appreciate his assistance and patience with my first book.

Unfortunately, because of the fact of where I live, there is not enough time to saltwater fish with everyone. However, friends like Chris Jay, Ed Opler, Joe Burke, Gary LaFontaine, Mike Lawson, Jake Jordan, Bruce James, Will Dornan, Mike Patron, and Brian Horn have been a great help over the years with advice and support on a career in fishing.

It would be nearly impossible to mention all the people and friends that had at least some influence on this book or my experiences fly fishing in saltwater. Those of you who are not mentioned know who you are, and I cannot thank you enough.

—JEFF CURRIER
May 1997

FOREWORD

IN EARLY NOVEMBER normal wind direction in the Caribbean can change, affecting everything from the fishing to insects. The insects were especially bad one evening as Jeff Currier and I prepared our tackle inside our island cabin in Belize. But the feeding sounds of husky horseye jacks pummeling outside our door to the ocean at Turneffe Flats were too tempting.

"I can't take it anymore, Jeff announced, grabbing a fly rod topped with a bulky Edgewater foam popper. "They've got to be stopped!" With that he bolted through the screen door, admitting about a million hungry sand flies and mosquitoes in the process. Jeff was clad only in a pair of Tarponwear shorts when he plunged after the marauding jacks. Within seconds I heard his reel drag blurting line as the first of the hungry jacks attacked his popper.

Casting personal comfort aside, I snatched a camera, figuring I'd better record the fun, despite the obvious risk of serious blood loss from the waves of insects. In the moonlight I could see Jeff's slender, shirtless body bent in combat with Mr. Horseye. He was applying the heat to this fish so he could tackle another one. Meanwhile, the bugs were applying their own version of "down and dirty" to us. Nobody in his right mind would have stayed out there enduring such an insect onslaught except a truly dedicated angler.

Jeff Currier brings this same sort of determination and enthusiasm to every project he tackles. Daily he sorts through waves of curious customers in the fishing department he manages, giving them as much information as possible to help their fishing vacations succeed. Meanwhile, he's always poring over maps and planning new adventures. Nightly his fly tying vise is a blur of activity. Frequently his innovations are the subject of my weekly newspaper columns.

Difficult conditions matter little when Jeff decides he wants to backpack into a remote part of bear-infested wilderness to nab a giant rainbow or leave home at 4 a.m. in sub-zero temperatures to tackle lake trout under the ice. Nor do civil wars, language barriers, transportation headaches and

The fish are in trouble as an extremely well-tackled Paul Bruun heads out on Belize waters.

skimpy information deter his quest for affordable saltwater fishing.

Jeff is always saving money and preparing gear for his next trip. He absorbs the difficulty of saltwater fishing travel happily, always setting a new goal for himself. He is generous with his information, eagerly encouraging and teaching the techniques he's found successful. I've been fortunate to join Jeff on some of his saltwater outings and we've always enjoyed ourselves. Whether it be sprinting after bonefish that were totally ignoring the annoyance of the 2-weight fly rod we were slinging, or admonishing wahoo and blackfin tuna that we chummed within casting range, time with Jeff Currier is rewarding.

I know you will enjoy the information he's assembled to help newcomers understand the thrill of saltwater fly fishing.

—PAUL BRUUN
Jackson, Wyoming
October 1996

INTRODUCTION

ALTHOUGH THERE IS AN ENORMOUS number of fly fishermen in the world today, only a small percentage have fly fished in saltwater. I have worked at the Jack Dennis Fly Shop in Jackson Hole, Wyoming, for over ten years and have been fortunate to meet thousands of fly fishermen from throughout the world. Some are envious of where I make my living, claiming that there is no fly fishing where they come from. For many this may be true, but, in fact, the majority of the population lives along sea coasts where saltwater fly fishing opportunities abound. Others tell me that they are aware of saltwater fly fishing near home, but have never tried the sport because they believe that it requires a lot of new and expensive tackle, or that the techniques and knots are too complicated.

The objective of *Currier's Quick and Easy Guide to Saltwater Fly Fishing* is to get you past these common misconceptions about the sport and to prime you with enough information to start fly fishing the salt. It is information that I have accumulated after years of on-the-water experience, learning from my own mistakes, and from experienced saltwater anglers and guides. I have explained and illustrated the various water types that you are most apt to fish, as well as the equipment, knots, and techniques that you will need to know to get started.

As you get further along in saltwater fly fishing, you will come to realize that there may be many ways to approach the same situation. For example, you will likely hear experienced saltwater anglers disagree about the proper way to strike a tarpon or the correct knot for a given situation, or even about the right brand of tippet material to use. In fact there are many ways to get to the same goal. In order to simplify things for the beginning saltwater angler, however, I have narrowed the scope of options to those that have worked for me. As you get further into the sport, you will likely want to experiment with other techniques and approaches; and you should. That's part of the fun.

WHY SALTWATER?

WITH ALL THE GREAT freshwater fishing throughout the world for trout, salmon, bass, pike, panfish, etc., why should you want to test your tackle against the harsh conditions of the world's oceans?

There are a number of good reasons. One is to escape the crowds that are often found at today's finer freshwater fly fishing destinations. There is lots more saltwater than there is freshwater on this planet. Therefore the options of where to fish are more plentiful. Easy-to-reach locations in the United States include the Atlantic Coast's popular Cape Cod, Montauk, Nantucket, or Martha's Vineyard islands of New England; Chesapeake Bay; the Florida Keys; and the coastline of the Gulf of Mexico stretching from Florida to Texas. Also, the Pacific Coast offers over one thousand miles of rolling surf and rocky points. Outside our borders, there are the exotic locations such as Belize, Costa Rica, Christmas Island, Australia, New Zealand, Papua New Guinea, and many more that provide outstanding fishing while allowing you to experience unusual cultures at the same time. All in all, the opportunity to fly fish remote, or even virgin, waters is nearly unlimited on the salt.

Saltwater also provides a more diverse selection of species from which to choose. How often can you cast into your favorite lake or stream and land more than a half-dozen different species in an hour? On the waters I regularly fish near my home in southeastern Idaho, it would probably never happen. However, I can recall landing thirteen different species ranging from barracuda to an unusual fly rod catch, a grouper-like jewfish, while fishing a Dahlberg Diver over

Matched size for size, saltwater fish are much stronger than their freshwater cousins.

some coral heads at Glovers Reef, an atoll off the coast of Belize.

The various saltwater species offer two more appealing character-istics as well—strength and speed—traits that have evolved as a result of being part of a lengthy food chain. The ocean is a dangerous place, even for the largest fish. For instance, three-foot barracudas are only hors d'oeuvres for the five-footers. A wounded or exhausted five-footer is just a morsel for an eight-foot hammerhead shark. Inch-for-inch and ounce-for-ounce, most saltwater species are stronger and faster than their freshwater cousins. My favorite way to describe how powerful they really are is to imagine a 20-inch rainbow trout tied tail-to-tail to an 18-inch bonefish. The rainbow would be dragged to the point of drowning within seconds as each fish attempted to swim in opposing directions!

Finally, saltwater will challenge all of your skills. Many situations re-quire you to spot a well-camouflaged fish and react quickly to their some-times fast, erratic, and unpredictable movements. You often have to make a long, accurate cast at the spur of the moment while the fish is within casting range. Ever-present winds contribute to the casting challenge.

Some larger saltwater species, such as giant tarpon or sailfish, require you to be in excellent physical condition to endure a lengthy battle. Finally, you need to know how to fight fish that take immediate high speed runs without breaking your leader. These are some of the challenges that turn saltwater fly fishing into such an exciting sport.

TIDES

ONE OF THE FIRST THINGS you will notice is the daily change in water level known as tide. For the most part, tides are created by the gravitational pull of the sun and the moon. The moon, because it is closer, influences the tides the most. Every twenty-five hours the oceans experience two low tides and two high tides.

Water flowing out of the bays and estuaries create the low tide. Then after a short pause known as the slack period, it pours back in and forms the high tide. The cycle from high tide to low tide is called a falling tide; from low tide back to high tide is a rising tide. These changes from low tide to high tide may be two to three feet in one place, and seven to eight feet only a short distance away. Variations found between two nearby locations can result from bottom contours and oscillations.

Location of the moon and the sun in relation to the earth affects the size of the fluctuation between low tide and high tide. The moon orbits the earth in approximately twenty-eight days. The greatest amount of gravitational pull occurs during the full moon and new moon when the sun and moon align directly with the earth. The tides at these times will be extra low and extra high and are called the spring tides.

When the moon and the sun do not align with the earth—which occurs during the first quarter and third quarter phases of the moon—there will be the least amount of gravitational pull. This is when the difference from low tide to high tide will be smallest and is known as the neap tide.

4

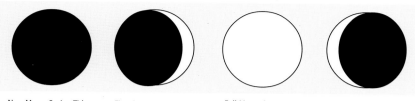

New Moon, Spring Tide   First Quarter, Neap Tide   Full Moon, Spring Tide   Third Quarter, Neap Tide

From spring tide to neap tide takes seven days. Every fourteen days the cycle from spring tide back to spring tide or neap tide back to neap tide occurs. Therefore, every twenty-eight days, the time the moon takes to orbit the earth, there are two spring tides and two neap tides.

The wind will also influence the level of tides. Picture an island at high tide. The windward side will have not only the normal level brought on by high tide, but also a slight increase brought on by the wind pushing along an excess of water. On the sheltered side or lee side of the island, the wind will not have this effect and the tide will be at normal levels.

The following will help you predict tides no matter where you are:

1. The moon rises fifty minutes later each day, thus the tides will occur approximately one hour later each day.

2. The size of the tide can be determined by knowing the phase of the moon and the direction and velocity of the wind.

Once you have an idea when the tides will occur, try to think about how it will affect the species you seek. Tides affect the food supply, and thus influence the movements of game fish. Unfortunately there is no specific rule for all species or for any particular bay or flat. Tides have a different effect on different species at different locations. For instance, take an area that completely loses water during low tide. During the high tide it could be covered by twenty-four inches of water and be ideal for bonefish or permit. On the other hand, a river mouth may fish perfectly for striped bass or bluefish along a New England coast during low tide. Game fish would likely be feeding on bait fish that cannot reach the cover of the salt marsh because of the low water. When high tide occurs, the increase in water allows the bait fish to retreat and hide, diminishing the game fish feeding opportunity.

This large striped bass was taken on a Lefty's Deceiver off a New England river mouth.

Does the fish you are after feed on bait fish or on crab and shrimp? Does it prefer shallow, warm, or clear water? After all these questions are answered, you are ready to pursue the quarry. When you can't answer these questions, a guide will be essential.

You do not always need to predict the tides yourself. There are many sources of information out there to give exact tide reports for most locations. A local tackle shop can be valuable. Chances are you will need to stop in for information anyway. While there, ask about the tides and you may be provided with a handy monthly tide chart for specific local areas. Coastal newspapers are another source for tide information, usually listing the exact times of both low and high tides for the upcoming day. Even computers can provide up-to-date tide information. There are tide programs available and there are at least two sites on the Internet. They are

Saltwater Tides: http://www.ceob.nos.noaa.gov/makepred.html; and Tide Predictions: http://tbone.biol.sc.edu/tide/sitesel.html.

If for some reason you end up on the water without information about the local tide conditions, then be creative. Pick a stick, marker, or rock and visually keep track of the water level. If the object is slowly being covered by water then the tide is rising. If a wet line continues to recede down the object, leaving it more exposed, then the tide is falling. Keep track of the exact time when the water level is lowest and highest, and, with the information you have already learned, you will be able to predict the tides on your own. This trick can be especially handy when fishing remote areas of the globe.

SIX TYPES 3 OF WATER

IF YOU ARE AN EXPERIENCED freshwater fisherman, you have seen the still waters of lakes and ponds as well as the moving waters of rivers. On a lake you have the option of fishing deep or shallow. If you choose deep water, sometimes baits must be presented along the bottom while other times your baits must stay above the bottom to reach suspended fish. When in shallow water, sometimes you fish over weeds, other times over rocks. It works the same on rivers. Sometimes you fish fast current, while other times you fish slow current. It all depends on what species of fish you are pursuing.

Options of where to fish in saltwater are similar, but, because of the vast expanse of ocean, there are more possibilities than just still or moving water. In fact, an entire book could be written on water types alone if it were to explain differences in places like rocky points and rocky shorelines. To keep things simple in this book, I will cover six different types of water that a newcomer to saltwater fly fishing is likely to encounter. These include river mouths and estuaries, surf, flats, channels, and coral reefs, all of which encompass what are considered inshore waters; and last, there is blue water, which is considered offshore.

This aerial view of Little Cayman Island shows many of the different water types.

River Mouths and Estuaries

ESTUARIES ARE FLOODED areas where rivers and bays pour into the ocean. They may consist of a mixture of fresh and saltwater known as brackish water. They provide excellent opportunities for fly fishermen. Because it is here that fresh and salt waters meet, I will discuss them first.

Estuaries always have current. A rising tide causes the current to head up river against its natural path, temporarily causing a slower flow. When the tide is falling, the river takes its natural course, rapidly pouring freshwater into the ocean and creating strong currents. Current is the main player in regulating the quality of fishing you find in these waters.

Generally, estuaries have a lot of structure, from both existing geographic features and years worth of debris that has been deposited by the river's flow. These are often great places to fish, because debris attracts fish, both big and small. The small fish, mostly bait fish, hide in the sunken debris, while the larger game fish come to eat the bait fish.

Bait fish are greatly affected by current. Bait fish do not have a home and avoid fighting tidal currents. The life cycle of many bait fish consists of being pushed by currents in and out of the rivers and estuaries in a consistent pattern, tide after tide. This pattern assures that game fish will find their daily meal.

Many saltwater species thrive in and around river mouths and estuaries. Striped bass is the best known, but you are also likely to find bluefish, snook, tarpon, jacks, channel bass, jewfish, mackerel, halibut, flounder, snappers, and sea trout, just to name a few, depending on the region and time of year.

During a falling tide when tidal currents are strongest, you will have the best fishing. At this time bait fish have the fewest places to hide because much of an estuary's structure becomes exposed. The current funnels the bait fish into certain areas. The game fish learn this pattern and wait in specific locations—under ledges or on the edge of sandbars—to ambush their prey. Finding these places can be as easy as exploring during a low spring tide. Remember their whereabouts, and you will find fish.

A striped bass storms a school of bait fish during low tide.

■ HAZARDS

Always be aware of potentially dangerous currents. Often at the point where a river mouth meets the open ocean, there is a natural collision of river flow and ocean current. Wind may increase the dangers to boatmen and wading fishermen. Boats can be overturned by strong wind pushing against a colliding current. While there are several examples of this, the one that comes to mind is the mouth of the Merrimack River in northern Massachusetts where I grew up. Avoid this type of water unless you are either familiar with the area or you are with a guide.

When wading around river mouths and estuaries, you must not only be aware of the strong currents, but also the drop-offs.

Particularly along the New England Coast, rock jetties frequently are built at river mouths to protect the integrity of the inlets. These can be great areas to locate fish, but they also can be dangerous. Slippery rocks can cause falls and rogue waves can wash even the most experienced angler into the water. Use extreme caution if you choose to fish from a jetty and select your footwear accordingly.

■ GENERAL FLY TACKLE RECOMMENDED

Unless fish are unusually big or winds exceptionally strong, the most practical fly rod is a 9-foot for either an 8- or a 9-weight line. Such rod weights have enough backbone to handle most species, even in strong current. Reels should have enough capacity for at least 150 yards of 20-pound backing along with a sturdy drag.

An intermediate or slow sinking fly line will be best for all-around estuary fishing. There are times, however, when a floating line will provide results. Most estuary-dwelling game fish feed on bait fish, so streamers will work best.

Wyoming guide Adam Cohen releases a bruiser snook taken from the Rio San Juan, Nicaragua.

Surf

THOUSANDS OF MILES of meandering, pounding foam borders the earth's land masses. Surf provides another playing field for the fly fisherman. At first, surf may not look like it would support fish. Turbulent water, with crashing waves and strong undertows can resemble a white water river. But, like its riverine counterpart, surf has nooks and crannies that hold fish. You will quickly learn that waves break over the shallow areas and roll over the deeper areas. These deeper zones hold calmer water that is hospitable to bait fish, crab, and seaworms, and, consequently, feeding game fish.

Fly fishing the surf is growing in popularity on the East, West, and Gulf coasts of North America. In the Northeast, the abundance of bait fish attracts schools of bluefish, stripers, and bonito during the summer and early fall. On the West Coast, surf perch, corbina, halibut, and calico bass hunt the shallows and kelp for sand crab and seaworms. Gulf Coast anglers catch snook, jacks, and mackerel.

While surf pounds the beach at Point Reyes National Seashore, careful observation reveals calm areas that, in turn, hold feeding game fish.

Surf fishing success is closely related to the tides. High tides are usually the most effective times to fish because of the increased currents. My best results come one hour before and then one hour after the high tide. It is during this time that depressions along the beaches hold the most water. Bait fish, sand crab, and seaworms are most stirred up when they are pushed into these depressions, where they become easy prey for feeding game fish. If you have limited time to fish, take advantage of the high spring tide and avoid fishing during neap tides.

■ HAZARDS

The best way to fish the surf is by wading, but when waves are crashing, expect to get wet. Waders and a rain jacket may be desirable depending on the climate and water temperatures where you are fishing. As you would at a river mouth, beware of currents. On a steep beach it is easy to have current or retreating surf knock your feet out from under you. This is especially dangerous while wearing waders and I recommend never venturing too far out in these circumstances.

■ GENERAL FLY TACKLE RECOMMENDED

Because the surf rolls up on the beach and sucks back out, any spare stripped fly line goes with it, making it difficult to make another cast. Don't be surprised when it even sucks the fly line out of the rod, pulling the fly to the rod tip! When this happens, sand from the beach will also get on the fly line. The combination of sand and tidal currents on your fly line will make it nearly impossible to cast. A stripping basket is the best solution to this problem. A bathroom-size waste basket or dish pan, strapped either in front of you or on your stripping-hand side, works well. Specially designed fabric or molded plastic stripping baskets are available from your favorite fly shop.

General tackle should consist of an 8- or 9-weight fly rod no shorter than 9 feet. I prefer a 9½-footer to allow a bit more clearance to back cast over beach and debris. The reel should have a minimum of 150 yards of backing and a good drag. In order to get the fly down in the surf, an intermediate sinking fly line works best.

Flies for the surf, like anywhere, depend on the location and fish you are after. Learn the habits of the fish. If a big striper is my goal, I fish streamers that imitate bait fish of the area. When after smaller quarry, crab flies and small shrimp patterns usually perform. Carry a variety of patterns when exploring unfamiliar areas.

The pristine flats of Christmas Island extend for many miles.

Flats

A FLAT IS A SHALLOW SAND or mud bottom area often covered by grass and mangroves with uniform depth. Because of the tide, depths will fluctuate. Some flats will be completely dry during low tide while harboring many fish during the high tide. Flats range in size from about one acre to several square miles. They can be found anywhere. Along the East Coast, they border river mouths, likely formed by accumulations of silt and debris poured out of the river over millions of years. They can provide great fishing during summer months for local species.

In the tropics, flats may border river mouths or surround islands and coral reefs, often randomly scattered throughout a region. Although striped bass are commonly sought among northern flats, the tropical flats are most heavily fished. The most commonly pursued flats feeder was once the bonefish, but with the growing interest in saltwater fly fishing, permit, tarpon, redfish, barracuda, and sharks are now popular prey.

While tides do affect the quality of fishing on a flat, the effect varies from location to location. One flat may fish better during the low tide while another less than a mile away fishes better during the high tide. Experiment on your own, or hire a guide to reduce some of the guess work.

Flats fishing requires hunting for fish more than blind casting. Once a fish is spotted, the stalk begins. Stalking a fish requires stealth, for if you are seen, the fish will likely flee to the safety of deeper water. Whether you are wading or being poled along by boat, ease your way towards the fish carefully and quietly. A quick movement or even just a shadow cast towards a fish can be enough to spook it. Once in range, a well-presented cast and the right fly are equally important. Seeking flats fish is more difficult than it sometimes appears because the fish, particularly bonefish, are difficult to see. Their reflective mirror-like sides enable them to blend in with their surroundings. Rely on certain hints provided by flats fish to locate them.

One of the easiest ways to locate fish is to find a mud. Water on a flat is nearly always clear because of the constant recycling of water that occurs from tides. A muddy or cloudy spot (the mud) in otherwise clear water suggests feeding fish. Most often either one or two fish or a small or large school of bonefish, permit, or other species are creating the mud while feeding voraciously along the bottom. Watch the mud to determine which direction the mudding fish are moving. Begin casting slightly ahead of the mud. Remember, there may be unseen fish foraging ahead. Finally, cast right into the mud, let the fly settle and start stripping. Chances are that at least one of these many fish will eat your fly, figuring that it is some type of creature that has been kicked up.

Searching for tailing fish is another method of working a flat. Tailing occurs when a fish's tail sticks up out of the water as the fish feeds

Flats fish can be difficult to see because their mirror-like sides provide excellent camouflage.

off the bottom. Bonefish, permit, redfish, and some snappers and jacks are famous for tailing while rooting the bottom for crab and shrimp. Sometimes striped bass can be found tailing at the edge of sandbars in northern waters. A tailing fish is a feeding fish and you should carefully plan your tactic. Determine the direction the fish is heading. Chances are that a good cast that leads the fish slightly will end with a strike. But remember, these tailing fish are in a vulnerable position and don't think they don't know it! Remember too, that there might be another fish feeding nearby that isn't tailing and you don't see. Study the situation. A sloppy cast is enough to send them running. The sight of tailing fish is an exciting one and can cause even the finest fly fishers to act too hastily.

Another method for spotting fish is to search for waking fish. The dorsal fin of a fish swimming near the surface will make a V-shaped wake that is visible on the surface. The fish will be slightly ahead of the wake. Wakes are easy to spot, but difficult to cast to because the fish is cruising. You must react quickly with an accurate cast. Always

The pale turquoise smudge on the water marks a huge mud moving along a flat at Little Cayman Island.

be sure to aim the fly to land far enough ahead of the fish so the fly may be seen. Do not cast at the wake. Instead of casting quickly, a common mistake is to not cast while waiting to identify the fish. Rather than asking, "What's that?" just cast. If it swims, try to catch it!

Another method of locating a fish is to search for nervous water. Both game fish and bait fish swimming or feeding near the surface can produce a riffle on the surface that looks different than the water surrounding it. It is by far the most difficult way to find fish because wind and current often create conditions that are similar. Handle nervous water just like a wake, with a quick and accurate cast. Never stare at it and wonder, "Is it a fish?" If the nervous water is moving along, lead your cast ahead of it. If it is not moving, then land the fly five feet off to one side of the disturbance, let the fly settle and strip. If you don't get a strike, cast again, each cast closer than the last, until the fly actually lands in the nervous water. On some days, flats fish seem to be extra spooky and will often avoid the shallowest part of the flats, never tailing or waking. On such a day, nervous water may be the only means of locating fish.

A tailing redfish is a common sight for most Gulf Coast anglers.

A final way to find flats fish is to watch for cruising rays and sharks. Frequently, game fish will follow these predators, picking up bait from bottom disturbances created by the movements of these larger fish. At times, redfish will move into an area frequented and disturbed by ducks resting on southern flats in winter.

■ HAZARDS

When most anglers think of fly fishing a flat they visualize wading, but flats with mud bottoms are like quicksand and are best fished by boat. The boats are known as skiffs or pongas and are designed to pass through shallow water. The most popular method of propulsion is known as poling. Canoes, sea kayaks and even prams or small inflatables can be used to reach many protected flats areas near shore.

Sand flats have a hard bottom and you can wade these. Sand flats are a favorite among fly fishermen. Often the sand bottom will contain

Two large bonefish create wakes as they cruise along a flat.

Nervous water is hard to detect. This photograph shows only a slight disturbance that moments later proved to be a permit (see arrow).

coral, broken shells, and a variety of damaging creatures such as sea urchins and sting rays. Footwear such as flats booties are a must in order to protect against these abrasive or stinging creatures. A sting ray tail can reach above booties. To avoid them altogether, shuffle your feet a bit between steps as you walk, frightening them out of the way rather than accidentally stepping directly on one. While fishing northern flats, you can wear waders.

Many days on the flats can be brutally hot, especially in the tropical latitudes. Heat exhaustion and even heat stroke are real dangers. Make sure you carry an ample water supply with you, and drink regularly.

A wise jack takes advantage of easy meals kicked up in the mud created by a ray.

■ GENERAL FLY TACKLE RECOMMENDED

The best fly rod for the flats is a 9-foot for an 8-weight line. On flats with obstacles like mangroves or coral, a rod of 9½ feet is better, allowing you to keep your fly line high enough to avoid obstructions while fighting a fish. As usual, the reel should have good capacity for line and backing. Due to the usually shallow conditions, a weight forward floating fly line is best.

A few specific flies will undoubtedly be needed on some flats at various locations throughout the world, but for the most part, choosing a flats fly pattern is not too difficult because most flats fish feed on shrimp, crab, and other small creatures like tiny minnows. Any fly that resembles these organisms is a good choice. One thing to keep in mind is that flats fish can be fickle. A well-balanced fly box is important. Although the fish you are after may feed on shrimp, you may need more than one shrimp pattern. Carry a variety of sizes and colors, and even a few different styles.

It doesn't hurt to carry a few streamers or poppers, either. We share our love of flats fish with other predators such as barracuda and sharks. On a day when bonefish may be scarce, sharks may be abundant, searching for the bonefish just like you. A popper on a short wire leader may give you more fun than you expected. Small sharks will gulp up a bonefish fly and put on a great show before they bite through your monofilament leader.

Channels

A CHANNEL IS A NARROW TROUGH of deep water cutting through shallow water, and is sometimes referred to as a cut. Channels, both natural and man-made, are often an integral part of river mouths and estuaries, and often separate flats, mangroves, and reefs. Regardless of location or how they were formed, they are ideal places to find large game fish. Channels are often easy to identify from a distance because of the rich blue or green color indicating depth. You nearly always find current in channels, and its force and direction is usually related to tides. Bait fish are constantly funneled through them and often gather along the edges and mouth. Species that normally inhabit the shallows often use them as a hideaway from predators from above, such as birds and fishermen. Larger predatory fish use channels not only as passageways to the shallows, but also as feeding stations.

You can fish a channel from the edge of a flat or salt marsh while standing in knee-deep water, but the best way is to slowly drift through it while casting from a boat.

Barracuda frequent "cuts" that border tropical flats as they wait to pounce on an easy meal.

Often, entrances to channels will be marked by channel markers or rock pilings. Always be sure to thoroughly cover these structures with some casts. Bait fish will often seek refuge here, attempting to dodge the current and nearby predator fish.

■ HAZARDS

Channels are generally safe places to fly fish because they are often sheltered from wind and large waves. Always be prepared for strong currents, however. Also keep in mind that because channels are often deeper than surrounding waters, you will likely be faced with other boat traffic. Be sure to be visible, and use common sense as to where you position your boat to avoid posing a hazard to other boat traffic.

■ GENERAL FLY TACKLE RECOMMENDED

Some of the largest fish I have ever taken on a fly came from channels. For that reason I never pass one by without a cast. At a minimum, I use a 9-foot rod for no less than an 8-weight; a 10-weight is even better.

Begin with a floating line. My favorite fly is a 2/0 popper. Almost every fish in the area comes to the noise a popper makes and usually one will strike. If nothing strikes, or if popper activity slows after I catch a few fish, I break out the sinking line and dredge the bottom with a large streamer or a Clouser Deep Minnow. Because most of my saltwater fly fishing experience has been in the tropics, the species I most often catch are barracuda and various types of snapper, shark, and jack. In channels of northern waters, however, it is common to find striped bass, especially during low tide.

Coral Reefs

A CORAL HEAD IS A LARGE PIECE of coral that grows from the ocean bottom towards the surface. Coral reefs are combined groups of individual coral heads, sometimes extending for hundreds of miles. They are found mostly throughout the earth's warmer oceans. They are living things that require a great deal of sunlight to survive. As a result they do not exist in deeper, darker water. They often separate deep water from the shallows by creating a barrier for islands and coastal land masses. They grow thick at the mouths of cuts where tidal currents dump into the blue water.

Reefs harbor more species of fish than any other water type in the ocean. Each coral head is like an apartment complex for fish, providing protective cover as well as a significant food source. The usual barracuda, sharks, and jacks are always present and willing to take a fly, yet it is the unusual species that make fishing coral reefs extra special. Grouper, snapper, triggerfish, boxfish, parrot fish, and many more will fight over your fly. Most of these fish can grow big. Really big! In fact, while in Belize, I once hooked a 4-foot barracuda that, while fighting at the end of my line, was swallowed by a giant grouper.

■ HAZARDS

Finding a way to safely fish a reef can be difficult. Boats are best, but huge rolling waves from bordering deep water often make it tough

An angler only gets a few casts between violent popper strikes from large trevally that patrol along the reef at Christmas Island.

to stabilize a boat for casting. Wading is difficult, but not always impossible. Water depth is key. Wear the toughest wading shoes available and be careful. Do not venture too far out, for it is easy to be swept away by powerful waves. If you were to fall or even just brush up against any of the coral, you would be badly cut and scraped on the coral's jagged edges. In fact, I highly recommend a guide for your first venture to the coral reef.

■ GENERAL FLY TACKLE RECOMMENDED

Use a heavy fly rod of 9 feet for at least 10-weight line. Coral is quite abrasive and any fish that gets the opportunity to take line and retreat to the coral head will probably sever your leader or even your fly line. The backbone of a big-game fly rod will enable you to prevent these powerful fish from retreating.

People often ask, " Why doesn't the leader break?" The answer is, that it will, unless you keep a strong bend in the rod, allowing it, rather than the leader, to absorb the stress of the fish's pull. Keep in mind that a smaller grouper —let's say 6 pounds— will make such a powerful run that even a 10-weight may not be enough to keep it from returning home to the coral head.

Use a floating line. In a water depth of 20 feet, the top of a coral reef may be only a foot or two beneath the surface. Coral can tear a fly line to shreds.

For flies I recommend poppers or unweighted streamers, again to reduce the risk of hang ups. Although not a lot is written about poppers, there is something special about an explosive popper strike from a coral-dwelling member of the snapper family. You'll have more fight than you bargained for, even from a modest size fish.

Blue Water

THE LAST WATER TYPE is probably the least fished by the fly fisher. This is the blue water, and although often located near the shallows of flats and coral reefs, it is the deepest water of the ocean. Blue water is often referred to as offshore fishing and it usually means big-game fishing. It includes species that were once unheard of on a fly rod, such as dolphin, tuna, wahoo, sailfish, and even marlin.

In blue water you cannot just pick up your fly rod and start casting and expect to catch fish. There is just too much water out there, and as on the flats, you must hunt. The most successful method to find game fish is to spot flocks of birds dive-bombing the water, feeding on leaping bait fish. This is a dead giveaway of the presence of game fish in a feeding frenzy. The bait fish are driven to the surface in an attempt to flee attack from below, unaware of the birds preying on them from above. When you see this situation, get as close to it as possible and cast your fly. Expect astonishing strikes! Although these game fish are the ultimate predators of the ocean, they still spook easily. Never drive a boat directly into the feeding area. This brings an abrupt end to the action.

Another method of finding fish in blue water is to locate floating structure such as weeds, logs, or buoys. Structure creates shade and works as a refuge for smaller fish. I have seen a single dead drifting buoy with a school of dolphin or small tuna around it. Weed lines are some of the most commonly found structure. Weed lines, mixed with other debris, will often extend for many miles. They are usually associated with current, and we should assume that bait fish are present. Larger fish lurk below weed lines, swimming them as if on patrol. Dolphin particularly love weed lines and will often be sitting just underneath the surface, waiting to pounce on something. That something should be your fly! Approach a weed line slowly, killing the engine before getting too close. Then, as you drift along, work the edges with casts.

Some days the action won't be so obvious. There will be no dive-bombing birds or weed lines to be found. The alternative is to attract fish. One way is to troll a teaser. A teaser is basically a lure or bait without hooks attached. Just like any trolling situation, at some point

The author's wife, Yvonne, proudly poses with a 50-pound yellowfin tuna taken from the blue water of Christmas Island.

you will pass over fish that will follow or even strike the teaser. When this happens, shift the boat into neutral and retrieve the teaser at a pace that keeps the fish hot on its tail. Present the fly on the water just as the teaser comes out, casting as close to the fish's head as possible. You want to get the fly in front of the fish before it either loses interest or is spooked by the boat. This is an effective method for billfish. When successful, it is gratifying not only for the fly fisherman, but also for the person manning the teaser.

Teasing fish also can work without trolling. Use a distance-casting spinning rod and a teaser lure to excite fish within casting range. Once these fish are worked up, pick up the fly rod and present them with either a streamer or popper.

Chumming is a proven method of attracting fish in blue water. It requires the use of whole or ground bait fish. It is best to cut up the bait fish into the smallest pieces possible, to emit a more potent slick in the water. Put the pieces into a small mesh bag, known as a chum bag, and hang it in the water behind the boat. Oils from the fish, and tiny flakes of flesh and scales will ooze from the bag. Continue to add fresh pieces to the bag in order to prevent breaks in the slick you've created.

If you have lots of chum, you can occasionally toss chunks overboard into your slick to further entice fish. Current and wind are important. Both will help to spread your slick through a large area. Although sometimes visible, the fish that arrive are usually too elusive to show themselves. Begin to cast and retrieve even before you see any sign of fish coming to the slick. Chum frequently attracts bait fish that, in turn, bring up bigger predators. Watch for explosions and boils behind the boat. Otherwise, remember that you are imitating chunks of dead bait fish rather than live, fast-moving bait fish. Use a fly to imitate these chunks, and retrieve it slowly. Be prepared to try several locations and different depths. Chumming requires patience, but it can be amazingly effective.

■ HAZARDS

Although the thrill of blue water can capture the interest of nearly any fly fisherman, not everyone can handle the big seas. Seasickness

Enormous flocks of birds dive-bomb leaping bait fish fleeing attack from below at Piñas Bay, Panama.

Captain Mike Kenfield holds a dolphin that devoured a popper.

has shortened many excursions and brought otherwise memorable days of fishing to a screeching, miserable halt. If you have never spent time on the rolling seas, then take medications such as Scopolamine, Dramamine, or even crystallized ginger, with you to help prevent sea-sickness. These precautions have allowed many fly fishermen to experience blue water fly fishing with a minimum of discomfort.

Also use common sense as to the type and size of boat used on blue water. Strong currents and huge rolling waves will be present even on the calmest of days. Always be sure that you have sufficient fuel and that motors are in perfect working condition. It is certainly a good idea to have a radio on board to be able to call for help in an emergency.

■ GENERAL FLY TACKLE RECOMMENDED

Blue water fish normally take flies well, and fooling them is usually easy. For that reason, fly patterns need not be too fancy. The challenge is landing them. Offshore fish are usually large and extremely powerful. They have the advantage over inshore fish in that there is lots of open space beneath them, giving them more room to maneuver.

Top: Sailfish teaser. Bottom: Sailfish fly. I recommend using a fly similar in color to the teaser.

You need a fly rod with great lifting power. An excellent all around choice is a 9-foot rod for a 12-weight line. Although the 12-weight is a little heavy for small tuna or dolphin, because the chance of a hook-up with a large fish is always high, it should be in hand. The reel must be equally as efficient, with a proven drag and substantial backing capacity. Consider having room for at least 300 yards of 30-pound backing.

I most often use an intermediate density sinking line. When fly fishing for billfish, however, I use a 30-foot sinking shooting head. The short length of the shooting head is easier to manage than the typical 80- to 120-foot fly lines as a blue water speedster rips it through waves.

This skipjack tuna came for the chum, but after being hooked, became a meal himself for a gray reef shark.

Tuna are extremely difficult to lift from the depths of blue water.

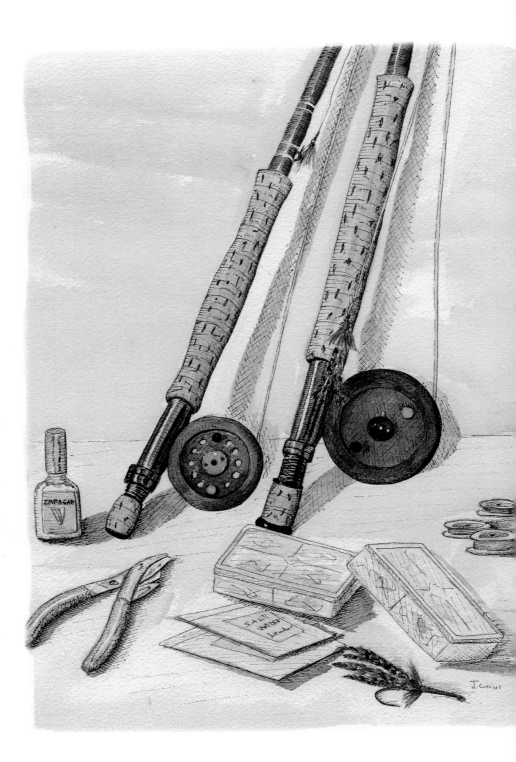

FLIES AND EQUIPMENT

THE COST OF A TOP QUALITY outfit often scares the potential saltwater fly fisher away from trying the sport. But if you have fly fishing equipment for freshwater, you may already have what you need to get started in the salt. Naturally I'm not recommending big game fishing with a 4- or 5-weight rod, but if you have an 8-weight, you're in business. Use your 8-weight freshwater tackle, be sure to wash it off thoroughly after each outing, and wait to buy your saltwater outfit only after you have learned more about the kinds of saltwater fly fishing that you will do most of the time.

Tackle choices abound for the saltwater fly rodder. You can start with a package containing rod, reel, and line, for $295 to $395. Or you can choose graphite rods crafted from the finest tapers available. Many saltwater reels are exquisitely engineered and cost upwards from several hundred dollars each.

Remember, despite substantial costs, modern equipment is an excellent value and most of it is guaranteed for life. Think in terms that you are making a worthwhile investment that will provide great satisfaction during frequent trips to your favorite saltwater destination.

Another legitimate concern is the complicated nature of some saltwater tackle. Chapter 3 provided general equipment recommendations for the various types of water. Now we'll examine the specifics of equipment selection. Gear selection can be simpler than you think.

Rods

IF YOU ALREADY FLY FISH, then technically you are ready for the salt because you have a fly rod. I've seen bonefish landed on 2-weights and tarpon beaten on 5-weights. But, as a practical matter, these rods are too light for most fishing conditions encountered in the salt. The ideal arsenal of fly rods would include a 9-foot for a 5-, 6-, or 7-weight, 9- to 9½-foot for an 8-weight, 9-foot for a 10-weight, and a 9-foot for a 12-weight. Since this would likely be too costly for the first salt venture for most anglers, wait on the 12-weight. This leaves three fly rods from which to choose: light, medium, and heavy action.

The 5-, 6-, or 7-weight rod may be a bit light for most situations in saltwater, but most freshwater fly fishermen may already have one of these. You never know when conditions will allow for its use. Imagine a day on the flats with almost no wind and 2-pound bonefish tailing everywhere. Your 8-weight fly line lands with such impact that nearly every bonefish you cast to spooks. Your only hope is to resort to the added finesse of your 5- or 6-weight. On your first cast the softness of your presentation rewards you with a hook-up, and after an exciting battle on such light gear, you land one. Light tackle can add a thrill!

An 8-weight is the most universal weight for saltwater fly fishing. It provides enough power to land anything from a nice size striped bass to a baby tarpon, while still being light enough to provide great fun fighting a small bonefish. I never leave the dock or beach without having my 8-weight on board, even in blue water. My favorite 8-weight is 9½ feet. A 9-foot rod is fine, but I find that the extra 6 inches comes in handy for lifting a back cast above obstructions behind me when surf fishing. The taller rod also hoists fly line over snags while fighting a flats fish. An 8-weight, just like a 5- or a 6-weight, is a rod that many freshwater anglers already own. If you find that you will be fly fishing primarily for fish like bluefish or bonefish, then a rod larger than an 8-

An 8-weight rod would be no match for this 90-pound giant trevally. The giant trevally is the largest member of the jack family.

weight probably isn't necessary. This is good news for your budget.

Many species, however, require larger than an 8-weight rod. A 9-foot for a 10-weight fly rod has the additional backbone needed to turn a big permit on a flat or lift a tuna from the depths of blue water. The 9-foot length is important. Additional length lessens the lifting power needed to pull a large dolphin or a stubborn jack from below the boat.

These three fly rod weights will cover most situations you are likely to encounter, but there is a place for an even larger rod. In recent years I have had the good fortune of being able to explore the challenges of blue water. My 10-weight rod was satisfactory on my first trip, but I now return with a 12-weight as well. Even larger fly rods that range all the way up to an 18-weight are designed specifically for fighting billfish and tuna. In fact, one of my most memorable fishing moments came while using a borrowed 18-weight and being connected to my first 100-plus-pound Pacific sailfish. I realized that day that there are many ocean fish that will never be landed on even the heaviest fly rod.

The spool of a direct drive reel spins wildly as a permit steals line.

Reels

A FRESHWATER FLY REEL rarely does more than store line. Strong drags and expanded backing capacities are available, but are not necessary. Saltwater changes these requirements. *At a minimum*, a saltwater reel should have:

1. A smooth drag able to endure repeated explosive runs.

2. Capacity for at least 150 yards of backing. Even more is necessary for some species.

3. Construction of corrosion resistant materials.

Three reel varieties are suited to saltwater: direct drive, anti-reverse, and the multiplier. The first two are single action and collect line at a 1:1 retrieve ratio. That is, every turn of the reel handle rotates the spool once. A multiplier collects line at approximately a 2½:1 ratio, a faster retrieval. The quicker retrieval sounds appealing, considering the long runs of many saltwater fish, but multipliers have many gearing parts to create this quick retrieve. More parts means more things that can break down. I recommend sticking with single action reels.

Both direct drive and anti-reverse fly reels retrieve line as the spool handle is rotated. They differ when the line goes off the spool. Each reel type has advantages and disadvantages.

As line leaves the direct drive reel, the spool and handle spin at the same rate as the line leaves the spool. That wildly spinning reel handle can hit your fingers, your shirt, chest, or stomach.

When line leaves the anti-reverse reel, the spool, but not the handle, spins, allowing you to hold the handle while the fish is running, just like a star drag conventional reel. Although you'll avoid smashed and bloody fingers, it's sometimes harder to know when to retrieve line again. Many experienced anglers prefer the extra drag feeling provided by the direct drive reel. Less experienced anglers frequently choose the anti-reverse system that avoids sudden break-offs caused accidentally by holding on to a reel handle that needed to spin.

Regardless of whether you choose a direct drive or anti-reverse reel, be sure it has a sound drag. Even with the most expensive and sophisticated reels, you will only need about three to four pounds of pressure. A major concern is drag smoothness. A fighting drag that flutters or is jerky can be a problem. Fluttering occurs when the drag sticks and releases as line is pulled off the reel. This can break off a nice fish. With a smooth drag, the line leaves the reel at a consistent pace, making it nearly impossible for a fish to break off. It is always a good idea to test the drags on your saltwater reels before a trip. Use a fishing scale to set the drag.

Make sure your reel has enough backing capacity. Most flats or estuary fishing requires a minimum of 150 yards of 20-pound backing. Bigger species such as giant tarpon or blue water speedsters can easily require a reel with a capacity of over 300 yards of 30-pound backing. The bottom line is simple. Big fish require a big reel.

Many saltwater reels feature stainless steel and anodized aluminum materials to help reduce corrosion from saltwater. But even anodization is not enough. *Clean your equipment after every day in the salt.* Reels require the most attention. An old toothbrush, a mild dish soap, and warm water should be used to thoroughly scrub every inch of a reel. Salt build up leads to rusting and reel failure during a critical battle.

Backing

BACKING IS THE FIRST LINE that goes on a fly reel spool. The two most commonly used line materials are either 20- or 30-pound test Dacron or Micron. Both of these lines stretch very little and lay smoothly on the spool. They resist mildew and rot, and dry quickly. The amount of backing and the choice of 20- or 30-pound test depends on the fish you are pursuing. For most of the inshore species, 150 yards of 20-pound is sufficient, and fits easily on any reel that suits an 8-weight fly rod.

For larger species of blue water fish or giant tarpon that may keep backing exposed during prolonged fights, 30-pound is a better choice. These larger fish often will run well into the backing, and much of the fight occurs at that time. Both Dacron and Micron can fray when violently rubbed against something like a crab line or speeding through the rod guides. The 30-pound backing holds up better than the 20-pound.

The recent introduction of high-strength thin-diameter braided backings made of a gel-spun polyethylene fiber called Spectra have expanded backing options. The super braids have amazing strength for their diameter. For instance, 30-pound test comes in the diameter equivalent to 10-pound monofilament (mono), allowing reels to fit three times the amount of backing on a spool. This may not be as good as it sounds. Under tension, thin lines have a tendency to dig into underlying line when peeled off a reel at a high speed. This can result in a momentary sticking or a backlash, and hence a break-off. For now, many experienced fly rodders are sticking with either Dacron or Micron because they have proven effective over time.

Fly Line

ALTHOUGH THERE ARE MANY DIFFERENT fly line tapers for fly fishing in general, there are only two types that belong in the salt, weight-forward (WF) and shooting tapers (ST). Both are designed to make quick casts. The weight-forward lines range anywhere from 82 to 120 feet in total length. "Weight-forward" means that the majority of the line's casting weight comes within the first 30 feet of line. The remainder of the line is a thinner running line, designed to slide easily through the rod guides.

Weight-forward lines are further divided into specialty lines such as saltwater taper, bonefish taper, tarpon taper, tropic plus blue water taper, and even billfish taper. Each of these vary in total length and in the amount of concentrated forward weight.

Some of these specialty lines are even formulated for the specific climate in which they are used. For example, the tropic plus or bonefish and tarpon tapers are excellent lines for fly fishing in hot climates. The core is made of braided mono and adds stiffness to the line keeping it from softening and wilting under the broiling tropical sun. These lines may be too stiff for colder climates. The best all around taper is the saltwater taper, which is designed for quick casting and driving bulky flies into the wind in all weather conditions.

Most saltwater fishing, whether in the California surf or in the tarpon waters on the Florida Gulf Coast, will require getting the fly below surface waves. If I were to suggest a single line, it would be a saltwater taper with an intermediate sink rate. A floating line is suitable for fishing on flats or working poppers, but the slight increase in depth gained by the intermediate line allows streamer flies to work better. Ideally you should have both floating and intermediate lines rigged on a pair of rods.

For blind casting—covering water and not casting to a specific fish—it is helpful to make long casts that explore a variety of depths. This is when shooting tapers (also called shooting heads) are nice. A shooting head is a 30-foot or less section of weight-forward fly line that is attached by a loop-to-loop system (illustrated in the knot section of the next chapter) to the end of the running line. Running line is a thin level fly line, 25- to 35-pound mono, or braided mono. The thin diameter of the running line creates little friction while traveling through a fly rod's guides. This allows for long casts.

Shooting tapers, like weight-forward fly lines, can be either floating or one of many sink rates. Most sinking shooting tapers are measured in grains. A 200-grain shooting taper (used on an 8-weight rod) is light and sinks at a slower rate than a heavy 800-grain taper (used on a 12-weight rod). Separate shooting tapers are not nearly as expensive as entire fly lines. A shooting taper system allows you to carry a variety of lines to attain a variety of depths. If you are really ambitious, you can make your own heads by cutting old full-length floating or sinking fly lines to the desired length.

Flies

FLIES VARY DEPENDING ON THE FISH you are after. As in freshwater, it is always best to use a fly that imitates whatever the game fish are eating. In Chapter 8 I list five favorite flies for a variety of saltwater species. You will notice that a lot of the same patterns are listed for many different species of fish, making your first saltwater fly collection much easier to build than you may have thought possible.

Additional Equipment

THERE ARE SEVERAL ADDITIONAL ITEMS which can be useful during your saltwater fly fishing experience. First of all, never go anywhere without sufficient rain gear. Have tops and bottoms even when fishing in tropical regions. If you are going to the tropics, take breathable fabrics such as cotton and wear light-colored, reflective colors. A hat and polarized sunglasses are essential to protect you from the sun and will remove glare from the water, allowing your vision to penetrate the surface.

Other items that you should not be without are a good pair of pliers that can be used to remove a hook as well as cut wire and heavy mono, a hook hone, a glove to handle fish with spines or abrasive skin, insect repellent, sun screen, drinking water to help prevent dehydration especially in hot climates, spare leaders and leader materials, and a small container of reel oil. Where you fish will determine whether you will need flats booties or waders, a stripping basket, flashlight, vest or fanny pack, and extra fly boxes.

Pliers are indispensable for any saltwater trip.

KNOTS

BEFORE MOVING ON TO LEADERS, let's learn how to set up the reel with backing and fly line. Knots have always been difficult for most anglers. However, knots keep you connected to the fish so you need to tie them to perfection. A variety of knots accomplish the same purpose. To keep it simple, I will illustrate one specific knot for each key point in your system. These key points are backing to reel spool arbor, fly line to backing, leader butt to fly line, tippet to leader butt, shock tippet to tippet, and the fly to tippet or shock tippet. With a little practice, you can master these knots. When you can tie them well, your overall fishing will improve.

Attaching Backing to Reel

FIRST YOU MUST ATTACH the backing to the fly reel spool arbor. A good knot is important here because in the ocean it is possible to have a fish run out all of your line and backing. Remember that if your knot was to break here, you would lose everything. I prefer to lose just the fly. The Arbor Knot is excellent for this first link.

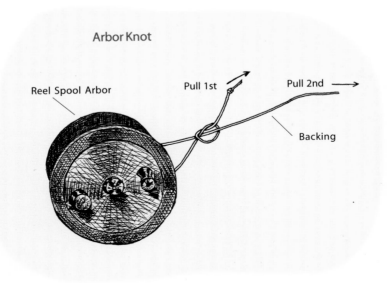

Arbor Knot

Reel Spool Arbor   Pull 1st   Pull 2nd

Backing

ARBOR KNOT

Step 1. Tie several Overhand Knots in the tag end of the backing. Wrap the backing around the spool arbor several times. Tie an Overhand Knot around the standing line and secure. Pull on the standing line until the knots meet tightly against the spool arbor.

Attaching Backing to Fly Line

BEFORE ATTACHING YOUR BACKING to your fly line, you need to learn how to make loops. A loop-to-loop system is by far the fastest way to make any connection. Therefore I use loops on the end of almost all of my fly lines. The first loop connection is where the backing meets your fly line. I make a loop in my backing with a Spider Hitch and a loop on the end of my fly line by Whipping a Loop.

SPIDER HITCH

Some anglers claim that the Spider Hitch is not as strong as a Bimini Twist. I have never experienced a breakage problem even while fighting large fish with the Spider Hitch. Also, the Spider Hitch is simple, taking less than 10 seconds, compared to the Bimini Twist, which takes nearly two minutes.

Step 1. Make a large loop about 20–25 inches in length out of the tag end of the backing. Near the base of this loop make a small reverse loop and pinch it between your thumb and forefinger.

Step 2. Be sure your thumb extends past your forefinger and the small loop extends past your thumb.

Steps 3. Wind the double line from the large loop around your thumb and the small loop six to eight times and pass the remainder of the large loop through the smaller loop.

Step 4. Now pull evenly to make the turns unwind off the thumb and tighten. The finished loop should be large enough to pass a reel spool through it.

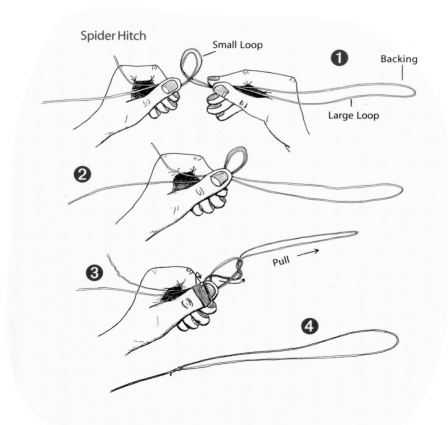

SPIDER HITCH WITH A SURGEON'S KNOT

I strengthen the Spider Hitch even further by creating a double line loop. This is done by making a Surgeon's Knot in the Spider Hitch loop.

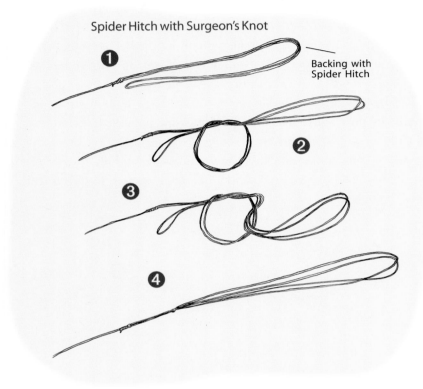

Spider Hitch with Surgeon's Knot

Backing with Spider Hitch

Step 1. Double back the end of the Spider Hitch loop against itself.

Step 2. Tie an Overhand Knot out of the loop.

Step 3. Make another pass through the newly created loop, making it a Double Overhand Knot.

Step 4. Pull tight.

Under great pull, the double line is stronger than a single line and is also less likely to cut through the opposing loop that it is linked with.

WHIPPING A LOOP

It takes nearly two minutes to whip a loop, but each fly line only needs two, one on each end. This is a strong knot.

Step 1. Trim the tag end of fly line at an angle as if creating a point. Fold it over to form a small loop approximately 1 inch in length.

Step 2. Take a bobbin with 3/0 or larger thread. Wrap the thread four times around the bobbin leg before threading. Hold the tag end of the thread against the looped fly line. Swing the bobbin hard, burying the thread into the finish of the fly line and binding the tag end of the fly line to the standing end.

Step 3. After you have a smooth connection, tie the thread off with several half hitches. Coat the finished loop with a soft drying glue such as Pliobond and allow to dry.

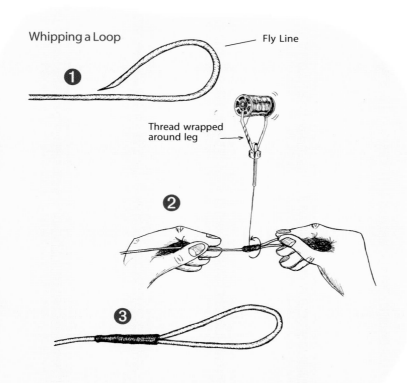

Whipping a Loop — Fly Line

① Thread wrapped around leg

②

③

JOINING THE LOOPS

In order for any loop-to-loop connection to maintain its maximum strength it must be linked correctly.

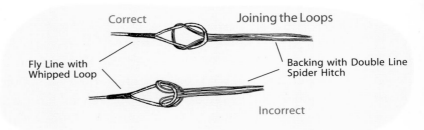

Leaders and the Rest of the Knots

THE LAST PART OF YOUR OUTFIT is the leader and tippet. The stiffness of mono leader materials is important to the proper performance of a saltwater outfit. There are soft, medium, and stiff monos available. Soft mono—the choice of trout anglers—is not a good choice for saltwater. Stiffer leader materials are necessary for turning over a leader with large flies. Leader abrasion is frequently a problem in saltwater, so tougher mono is necessary. I recommend using any of the popular saltwater leader materials such as Climax II Saltwater, Orvis Mirage, Ande Tournament, Jinkai, or Hard Mason .

Three different types of leaders will be discussed throughout the remainder of the book—Type A (Basic Heavy Duty Leader), Type B (Custom Class and Shock Tippet Leader), and Type C (Toothy Critter Leader).

TYPE A LEADER

A Type A leader is the simplest, and resembles a normal freshwater leader, only it's heavier duty. It is the only leader that I would recommend purchasing pre-made. It is basically a knotless tapered leader of specific length and tippet strength. It is used for species

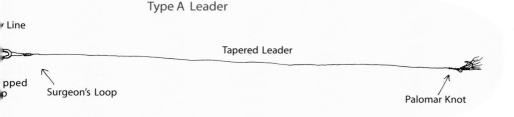

Type A Leader

Line

Tapered Leader

pped
o

Surgeon's Loop

Palomar Knot

such as bonefish that do not have tippet cutting sharp teeth or abrasive gill plates or skin.

You only need two knots when using a store-bought, pre-made Type A leader, Surgeon's Loop, for attaching the leader to the whipped loop on the end of the fly line, and a Palomar Knot for tying on the fly. Here is how you tie them.

SURGEON'S LOOP

A Surgeon's Loop is the easiest leader loop to tie. This loop quickly allows a leader change and it is strong.

Step 1. Double back the tag end of the leader butt against the standing line and form a loop approximately six inches long. Tie an Overhand Knot out of the loop, but don't pull tight.

Step 2. Make another pass through the newly created loop, making a Double Overhand Knot.

Step 3. Pull tight.

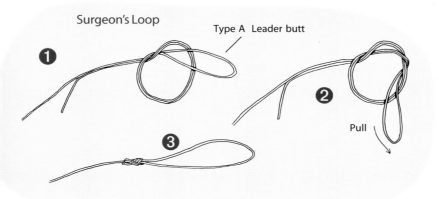

Surgeon's Loop

Type A Leader butt

Pull

PALOMAR KNOT

Although the Palomar Knot uses up more tippet than most knots, it is strong and simple to tie.

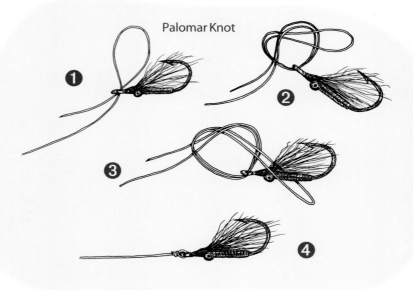

Step 1. Make a loop at least four inches long at the end of your tippet. Pass the loop through the eye of the fly.

Step 2. Tie an Overhand Knot with the loop around the standing end and the leader tag end.

Step 3. Pass the fly through the loop and pull the leader gently until it completely clears the fly.

Step 4. Continue to pull the tag end and standing line while holding the fly firmly until the knot is snug.

Unfortunately the Type A leader is not the best choice for most saltwater species. Many of these fish have mouths and skin like sand paper, sharp teeth, or gill plates that will easily wear through even 20-pound tippet during a battle. Therefore, Type B leaders are necessary.

The abrasive mouth and sharp gill plates of the tarpon require the use of a mono shock tippet.

TYPE B LEADER

Learn to build the Type B leader yourself and do not purchase it pre-made. It consists of three separate sections—the butt, class tippet, and shock tippet. The shock tippet is the last section and is made from a heavy piece of mono or wire no more than 12 inches long. In the case of the Type B leader, we will consider it to be mono. Its strength can range anywhere from 30- to 150-pound test. The larger your quarry, the heavier the shock tippet may be.

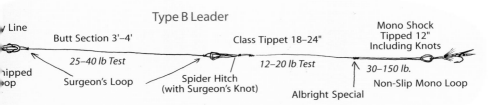

Type B Leader

y Line

Butt Section 3'–4'   Class Tippet 18–24"   Mono Shock Tipped 12" Including Knots

ipped op   25–40 lb Test   12–20 lb Test   30–150 lb.

Surgeon's Loop   Spider Hitch (with Surgeon's Knot)   Albright Special   Non-Slip Mono Loop

The class tippet is the section between the butt and the shock tippet and is made of weaker test than the shock tippet. Anglers often ask, "If a fish will eat the fly while attached to the heavy shock tippet, why even have a light class tippet section in the middle?" The answer is that a leader must have a section that is of a weaker test than the backing and fly line to prevent the loss of an entire fly line.

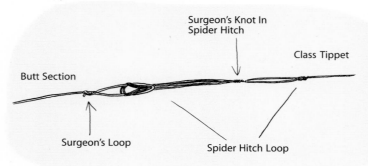

Notice how the butt section and the class tippet are looped together. Each uses a different knot. The butt section has a Surgeon's Loop while the class tippet has a Spider Hitch with a Surgeon's Knot in it, thus creating the double line.

Two new knots are necessary for the mono shock tippet—the Albright Special for attaching the shock tippet to the class tippet; and the Non-Slip Mono Loop for attaching shock tippet to the fly.

ALBRIGHT SPECIAL KNOT

Step 1. Tie a Spider Hitch in the end of the class tippet that will attach to the shock tippet. Create a tight bend in the end of the mono shock tippet that will attach to the class tippet. Push the Spider Hitch loop of the class tippet through the shock tippet bend. Keeping the bend in the mono shock tippet, hold the loop from the Spider Hitch firmly between your thumb and forefinger.

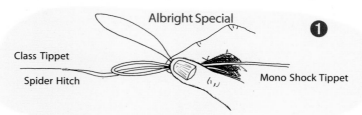

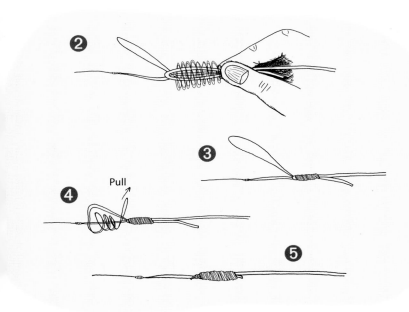

Step 2. With the Spider Hitch loop, make 10 wraps toward the bend in the shock tippet and push the end of the Spider Hitch loop back through the shock tippet bend, the opposite direction of where it originally entered.

Step 3. Pull gently to tighten the wraps around the shock tippet bend and carefully slide them towards the closed end. Do not let any slide off.

Step 4. Before trimming the excess of the Spider Hitch loop, form a lock above the Albright with a triple half hitch on the class tippet.

Step 5. Tighten.

NON-SLIP MONO LOOP

A fly tightly knotted to shock tippet has less swimming action because of the stiffness of the heavier material. The Non-Slip Mono Loop allows the fly to swing freely on the loop.

Step 1. Before attaching the fly, make an Overhand Loop in your shock tippet material three inches back from the tag end to which the fly will be attached.

Step 2. Run the tag end through the eye of the fly and up through the Overhand Loop, entering the loop on the same side the tag end exited.

Step 3. Wrap the tag end around the standing line two to three turns and insert the tag back through the Overhand Loop (heavier material requires fewer turns).

Step 4. Moisten the knot and work into place with pliers by pulling lightly on the leader tag end and pulling harder on the hook.

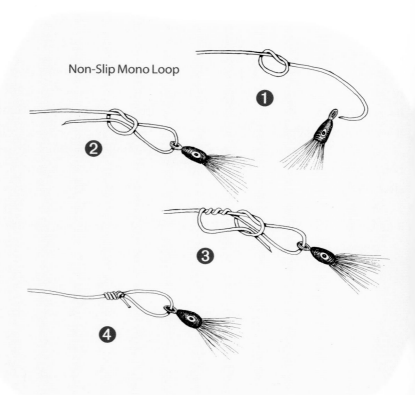

Non-Slip Mono Loop

A NOTE ABOUT SHOCK TIPPET

Shock tippet is stiff and holds a great deal of spool memory, usually in curls. To prepare it for easier use, take 20 feet of shock tippet from its spool. Cut it into 18-inch sections and dip them in boiling water. When removed they will be limp. Dry the sections in a straightened position and store until needed in a 19-inch piece of ½-inch diameter PVC tubing marked with the pound test. PVC tubing is available at most hardware stores.

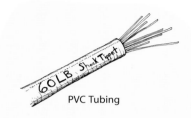

PVC Tubing

TYPE C LEADER

The last leader, a Type C, includes wire shock tippet. As with the Type B leader, you should build this yourself. It is for fish with sharp teeth, such as bluefish, shark, king mackerel, and barracuda. Because their teeth can easily shear through heavy mono, you need wire shock tippet. There are two types of wire available—braided and solid. Braided wire is a group of intertwined light, solid wire strands. It is easy to tie in knots because it is pliable, but I have had sharks gradually bite through each individual strand, finally breaking the shock tippet. I have since converted to solid wire for toothy fish. Solid wire is a single strand of wire. I find that 40-pound test is sufficient for most fish. Place a swivel between the class tippet and the wire. Flies attached to wire often twist, causing kinks which will quickly destroy your leader. The swivel will reduce, if not eliminate, this problem.

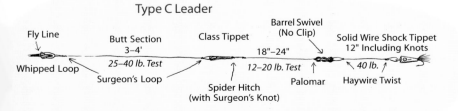

Type C Leader

Toothy fish such as this barracuda require a wire shock tippet.

The only new knot here is the Haywire Twist. It attaches the swivel and the fly to the wire shock.

HAYWIRE TWIST

Step 1. Place the tag end of wire through the eye of the fly or swivel. Form a loop and cross the tag end over the standing wire. Hold the loop tightly between your forefinger and thumb.

Step 2. Twist the tag end of wire and standing wire together, while holding the loop securely in the other hand. This should form twists that look like X's. Do at least four of these.

Step 3. To secure the knot, make six to eight more tight wraps with the tag end over the standing wire. To begin this maneuver, first bend the tag end so that it is at a right angle to the standing wire. Then wrap.

Step 4. When the wraps are completed, bend the tag end back and forth until it breaks off. Never cut the tag end off with pliers, for that will always leave a jagged edge which could damage other parts of your leader.

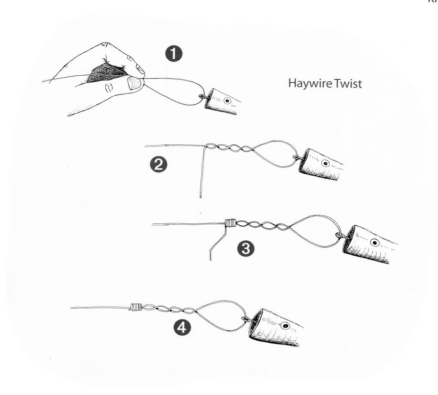

Haywire Twist

Although I always use a swivel, some anglers do not like to use a swivel between their class tippet and wire because it adds weight and wind resistance to the leader. If you choose not to use a swivel, or if you don't have one, you can use the Albright Special to attach class tippet to wire.

A Note on Type C Leaders

You will notice that the Type C leader is difficult to cast. If you keep it short, it will cast easier. Most of the time, a fish that will take a fly attached to wire isn't frightened by the fly line. You can eliminate the butt section altogether and fish with a leader of less than 3 feet. Also, use the shortest piece of wire that you can. For sharks, which are usually lip hooked, I use less than six inches of wire between the class tippet and fly. Other fish that inhale flies, such as barracuda, require a full twelve inches of wire.

Tips on Knots

1. Once you have completed your knot, but before you have tightened it, moisten your knot so it slides together with less friction, reducing its loss of strength.

2. Use pliers to tighten all knots involving heavy mono shock tippets. You cannot tighten them sufficiently by hand.

3. When trimming a knot, remember that mono will shrink and expand with temperature. Do not trim it so closely that it will likely unravel.

4. Test all completed knots with a solid consistent tug. Loops should be tested by inserting a smooth object in them and pulling firmly.

5. If you are concerned with an IGFA record, Type B and C leaders have some required specifications. The class tippet must be at least fifteen inches long from the connecting knots and the shock tippet may not exceed twelve inches including the knots.

6. Pre-tie your class tippets before going fishing. Tying the class tippet to the shock tippet is easy, but time consuming. Imagine yourself on a week long adventure, the trip of a lifetime in a remote location such as Belize. Fishing for tarpon has been slow, but because of your persistence, the opportunity to cast to a school finally comes. You hook up, but in your excitement you break off your fly within seconds. The rest of the school remains and surely one would take another fly. The problem is that by the time you re-rig they will be gone.

What if these knots were already done? When I purchase a spool of tippet, perhaps 15-pound test, I pull it all off. I then cut it into 30- to 40-inch sections and tie a Spider Hitch on every loose end. When completed, I loop-to-loop all the class tippets together, stretch them across the room and touch the knot of each loop with zap-a-gap glue. When dry, I wrap them all back on the original spool.

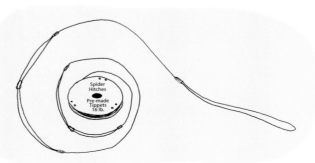

Next, I pull off sections of my class tippet, add on the shock tippets, either mono or wire, and tie on the flies. Then I take a stretcher box, a box designed to hold tippet sections with shock tippet and the flies already attached, and load it with as many as it will hold. To accommodate for minute differences in shock tippet lengths, I use rubber bands to secure the fly. Fully loaded, this box is almost as important as my fly rod and reel outfit itself. Now, while in the midst of fish, from tarpon to sharks, I can change flies in seconds by pulling out a pre-made tippet already connected to shock tippet with fly attached, and loop it onto the butt section of my leader or the end of my fly line.

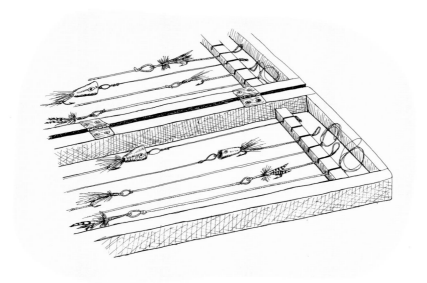

SALTWATER 6 FLY CASTING

. . . . . .

FLY CASTING IN SALTWATER is much more demanding than in freshwater. The fish move quickly and require longer casts. Also, the wind is often strong, making it difficult to get the fly accurately to the fish. If you already cast well in a freshwater setting, you simply need to expand your skills with a larger rod to add distance and speed to your technique. This chapter will elaborate on the Double Haul, which, when mastered, will add the needed speed and distance to your cast. Accurate casts of sixty to one hundred feet will allow you to catch more fish.

Whether you use a Double Haul or a Single Haul, it is important to get off a good cast quickly. Cruising fish are often in casting range only briefly, so you need to cast immediately, before the opportunity is lost.

First, have the fly line ready to shoot. Pull as much fly line off the reel that you are likely to cast or can handle comfortably. Remove the line's memory by stretching it between your hands or by tying it to a stationary object and pulling. Make a practice cast and retrieve the line back, dropping it either into a stripping basket or on the boat deck in large coils. The line is now in the proper order to make a cast. Move or cover any obstacles like coolers, tackle boxes or gear bags that the line could catch on during casting.

Hold the rod in your casting hand and the fly in your line hand while awaiting the arrival of a fish. Have at least ten feet of fly line outside the rod tip so that when starting into a cast, there is enough line weight to load the rod. The more line handled beyond the rod tip, the more quickly you can fire off a cast. Now you are ready.

Next comes the cast itself. In order to cast quickly, minimize your number of false casts. Ideally you should be able to cast sixty feet in three false casts and anywhere between eighty and one hundred feet with a fourth. You can achieve this with the Double Haul. The Double Haul increases line speed, thus reducing the number of false casts necessary to reach your distance. An eighty-foot caster has a fish within range for a longer period than a sixty-foot caster. The eighty-foot caster can probably cast sixty feet straight into the wind. The Double Haul is essential and, luckily, easy to learn. This is how it is done.

Double Haul

THE SKETCHES ON THE FACING PAGE SHOW a complete cycle of one false cast using the Double Haul technique.

I recommend that you practice the motions with just your hands and a pencil until you feel comfortable. Get the rhythm down in slow motion first and increase speed gradually until you attain a normal false casting pace. Finally, add the rod, reel, and line and try the technique in your back yard. Most anglers who master the Double Haul use it routinely, even with lighter rods on smaller waters.

Step 1. Begin the cast with the rod tip close to the water. Strip in any slack in the fly line. This will allow for a powerful pick-up and back cast which will load the rod efficiently from the beginning.

Step 2. As you start the back cast, simultaneously jerk the line hand downward just a few inches. This rapid line hand movement increases both line speed and the loading of the rod. This is the first of two line speed building movements called the "haul."

Step 3. Quickly return the line hand close to the rod hand where it remains during the pause between the back cast and forward cast.

Hold the fly line tightly and prepare for the second portion of technique.

Step 4. At the start of the forward cast, simultaneously jerk the line hand downward again. This second haul again increases line speed and the load in the rod.

Step 5. Again, the line hand returns close to the rod hand during the pause between forward cast and back cast. This time, while controlling with the line hand's thumb and forefinger, allow line to slide out, lengthening the false cast. Then when the maximum release of line is attained, close your line hand tightly on the line and repeat the entire process until the preferred casting distance is reached.

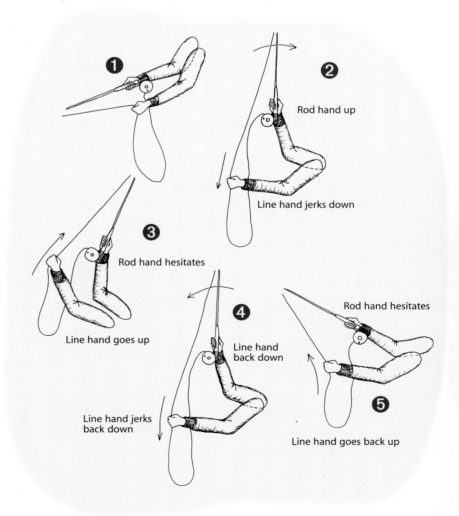

1. Hold the line tightly. The increased speed and loading from the haul often causes the line (especially when wet) to slip through your fingers too soon.

2. A powerful haul-aided forward cast often kicks the accelerating line around rod butt or reel. To avoid this, upon delivering the fly on your final cast, guide the accelerating fly line while it slips through your line hand. This will prevent tangling and allow you to start stripping as soon as the fly settles on the surface.

3. Your casting will be affected by leader length, fly size, and wind directions, among other things. Add the excitement of seeing a fine fish and realize it takes practice and experience to manage all these elements. Remember that larger rods, lines and flies take a little more time and effort to develop the same casting dynamics you are familiar with in lighter tackle. Be patient with yourself.

Shooting Line on the Back Cast

ALTHOUGH THE DOUBLE HAUL is the most powerful method of casting saltwater fly equipment, another way to make a quick cast presentation is by letting a few feet of line slip out of your hand during the back cast. You can do this when making either a Single Haul or a Double Haul cast. The additional bit of airborne line increases the loading of the rod while also reducing the amount of line needed to shoot on the forward cast.

Start by letting only a foot or two of line loose. Shooting too much line at first will hurt your timing and may bog down the forward cast.

7
HOOKING AND LANDING FISH

AFTER A FEW SALTWATER OUTINGS, you'll recognize the importance of good fly casting. You will also appreciate the importance of accurate casting, especially when fishing for certain species. For instance, the fly must land close to the eyes of redfish and sharks in shallow water for them to strike best. On the other hand, bonefish and snook have excellent vision and can spot a fly from quite a distance, and will spook when a fly lands too close. This is true of many other species as well. In either case, a good cast with the right fly is often followed by a strike. Once you've made the good cast and drawn the strike, there is more you can do to improve your odds of landing the fish.

It is common practice on a trout stream to set the hook on a dry fly by raising the rod tip up over the shoulder as if to back cast. In saltwater the hook-set is done differently. Ocean fish often travel in schools. When a fish strikes, it is often because it was the first of several to get to your fly. An over-the-shoulder hook-set that does not make contact pulls the fly away from the feeding fish. Instead, you need to set the hook by stripping until you feel the fly hooking the fish and then drive the hook deeper by jerking the rod to the side. Should the fly pull free, it is still in sight of the missed fish as well as the others that might be following. You'll have a second chance. For soft-mouth species like bonefish, this combination of a strip and rod jerk should hook the fish sufficiently to land it. For hard-mouth fish like tarpon, aggressively repeat the rod jerk several times.

Once you have hooked the fish, you must properly play it in order to tire it for landing. The initial run of most fish is fast and furious. Hold the rod tip high and allow the fish to go. Loose line that was stripped in before the strike will leave the boat deck or water at the same speed as the fish. If it catches your reel or rod butt, you'll lose the fish. Be sure it has a clear path in which to leave by guiding it away from the reel and rod butt with your line hand. To avoid the line cutting or burning you, don't grip the line too tightly.

If the fish jumps, drop the rod tip toward the fish to create slack in the line. This maneuver is called bowing. The weight of some of these bruisers falling on the line or leader is enough to break a tippet.

The reel drag, as well as trailing fly line and backing, will begin to tire the fish. When the fish slows or stops, add pressure by increasing

A healthy bonefish waits to be released.

the bend in the rod. Gain back all the line possible using a smooth pumping motion. Lift the rod firmly, then move the tip back toward the fish and reel in the slack repeatedly. Pinch the line with your rod hand while reeling with the other hand. Try to guide the backing and fly line evenly onto the reel.

The key to the fastest possible landing is to continue to add pressure on the fish, often changing the angle of the rod. This causes the fish continuously to change its angle to you, never allowing it a moment's rest. Be prepared to let the fish run again whenever you feel a sudden surge. A five-pound bonefish may take fifteen minutes to land for a beginner while the more experienced angler lands it in five. A fish landed in five minutes as opposed to fifteen has a much better chance of surviving after release. Keep the pressure on!

POPULAR SALTWATER GAME FISH

WHAT FOLLOWS ARE A LIST of seventeen commonly sought-after saltwater species with color illustrations so you can identify them immediately. Listed with each species is the water type in which they reside, precautions to consider when handling that species, recommended tackle, and five effective fly patterns to catch them.

Bonefish

Notes: One of the most commonly sought after shallow-water game fish.
Water Type: Flats.
Size: Commonly in the 2- to 4-pound range. Large fish in the 9- to 14-pound range frequent the Florida Keys and Bahamas.
Food Preferences: Shrimp, crab, mollusks, and small fry
Handling Concerns: Beware of crushers in rear of the mouth that are used for crushing the shells of crab and other crustaceans. Do not put your finger into their throats.
Recommended Tackle: (Based on a 4- to 8-pound bonefish)
 ROD: 9- or 9½-foot for an 8-weight line

REEL CAPACITY: 150–200 yards of 20-pound backing
LINE: 8-weight floating—WF8F
LEADER: Type A, 9- to 12-foot, 8-pound tippet
FLIES: The best hook sizes range from 8 to 2 and favorite colors are tan, white, pink, green, and yellow. Excellent patterns include the Crazy Charlie, Snapping Shrimp, Nix's Epoxy Fly, Clouser Deep Minnow, and the McCrab. Check on preferred colors of the area you'll be fishing before you get there, and stock up on those colors.

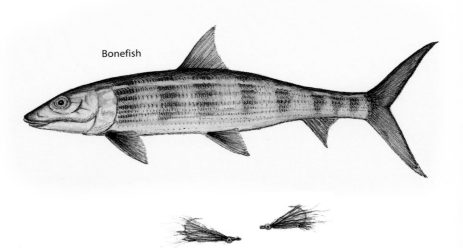

Bonefish

Crazy Charlie Flies

Permit

Notes: Because they are wary, elusive, and selective, a permit on the flats may be the most highly prized fly rod game fish in the world.

Water Types: Flats, reefs, and shallow wrecks

Size: Average 8 to 12 pounds, can reach over 50 pounds

Food Preference: Crab

Handling Concerns: Beware of crushers in rear of the mouth that are used for crushing the shells of crab. Don't put your finger into their throats. They are easy to grab at base of the tail, but use a glove because of abrasiveness on large fish.

Recommended Tackle: (Based on a 10- to 25-pound permit)

ROD: 9-foot for a 10-weight line. Use a heavier rod, up to 12-weight, if you fish around wrecks.

REEL CAPACITY: 200–300 yards of 20- to 30-pound backing

LINE: 10-weight floating—WF10F

LEADER: Type A, 9- to 12-foot, 12-pound tippet

FLIES: The best hook sizes range from 6 to 1/0. Colors should resemble the crab in the area you are fishing. Excellent patterns include the McCrab, Del's Merkin Crab, Nix's Epoxy Fly, Clouser Deep Minnow, and the Crazy Charlie, which has fooled lots of permit when they appeared while anglers were bonefishing.

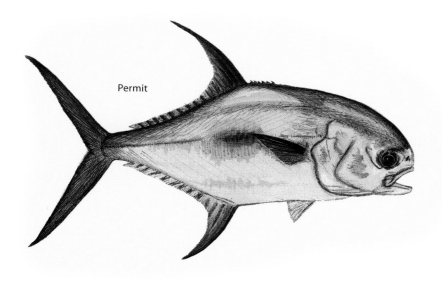

Permit

McCrab Fly

Del's Merkin Crab Fly

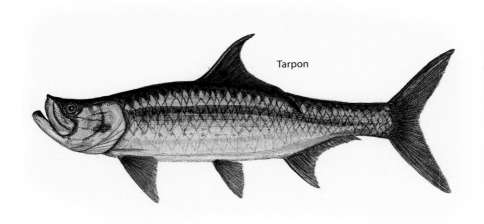

Tarpon

Tarpon Glo FLy

Tarpon

Notes: A favorite fly rod species. Tarpon are willing strikers that fight hard and excel as acrobats.

Water Types: Flats, rivers and estuaries, and channels

Size: The term baby tarpon refers to 10- to 60-pounders with giants considered to be over 120 pounds. They may exceed 200 pounds.

Food Preferences: Mullet, pinfish, and other various bait fish, squid, shrimp, worms, and crab

Handling Concerns: Be aware that a hooked tarpon can jump into the boat and injure your tackle and you. Gaffing large tarpon is a serious maneuver and there are numerous stories of anglers being pulled overboard by larger fish. Gill plates, scales, and mouth are all sharp and abrasive. Remember, aggressive sharks prey on tarpon and frequently inhabit the same waters where tarpon schools travel.

Recommended Tackle: (Based on a 60-pound tarpon)

ROD: 9-foot for a 10-weight line

REEL CAPACITY: 200–300 yards of 30-pound backing

Line: 10-weight floating—WF10F or 10-weight intermediate sinking—WF10I

LEADER: Type B, 9-foot, 12-pound tippet, 60-pound mono shock tippet

FLIES: The best hook sizes range from 1/0 to 4/0. Orange combined with grizzly is my favorite fly color combination, but any color or combination works at the right time. The best patterns include the Tarpon Glo, Lefty's Deceiver, Blanton's Whistler, Cockroach, and Sanchez Double Bunny.

Snook

Notes: Snook are opportunistic and aggressive feeders that ambush their prey, usually from protected areas. They especially like structures such as dock posts, tree roots, and brush. Snook can be moody feeders, refusing every fly you try one day while falling easily for the

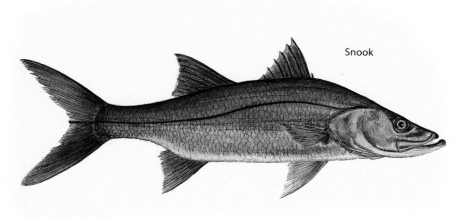

Snook

Dahlberg Diver Fly

same patterns on a different tide or the next day. Snook are nocturnal feeders and seem to strike well on overcast, rainy days.

Water Types: River mouths and estuaries, surf, bridges, seawalls, docks, channels, mangrove shorelines, and drop-offs affected by substantial tidal flows

Size: Commonly ranges from 8 to 25 pounds, can exceed 50 pounds

Food Preferences: Mullet and other various bait fish, shrimp, and crab

Handling Concerns: Be careful of the razor-sharp bone on the gill plates.

Recommended Tackle: (Based on a 10-pound snook)

ROD: 9-foot for an 8-weight line

REEL CAPACITY: 150–200 yards of 20-pound backing. Long runs are unlikely, but a reel with a good drag will help to keep a snook from retreating to its home among the mangrove roots.

LINE: 8-weight floating—WF8F

LEADER: Type B, 9-foot, 15-pound tippet, 50-pound mono shock tippet

FLIES: The best hook sizes range from 1/0 to 3/0 and a wide variety of colors and combinations work, with my personal favorites being yellow, orange, and red. Excellent patterns include the Lefty's Deceiver, Clouser Deep Minnow, Tarpon Glo, Dahlberg Diver, and poppers.

Striped Bass (Striper)

Notes: Although they are not known to jump or take high-speed runs, they are one of the most popular saltwater game fish.

Water Types: River mouths and estuaries, surf, flats, and channels. Stripers have also adapted well after being introduced to freshwater lakes and rivers throughout the southern United States.

Size: 20-pounders are abundant, but they can exceed 60 pounds

Food Preferences: Herring, silversides, and other various bait fish, sand eels, squid, shrimp, and crab

Handling Concerns: Beware of dorsal spines, and sharp gill plates and rakers

Recommended Tackle: (Based on a 20-pound striper)

ROD: 9-foot for a 10-weight line

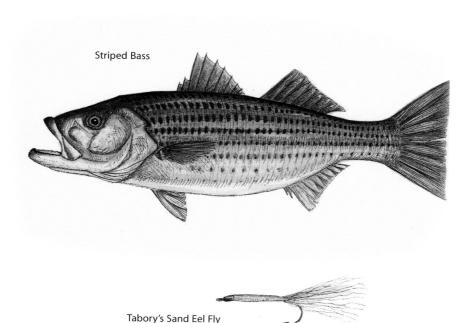

Striped Bass

Tabory's Sand Eel Fly

REEL CAPACITY: 200–300 yards of 20- to 30-pound backing
LINE: 10-weight intermediate sinking—WF10I
LEADER: Type A, 9-foot, 15-pound tippet
FLIES: The best hook sizes are 1/0 to 5/0 and a favorite color is white, often combined with olive, black, or brown. Excellent patterns are sparsely tied, and include Tabory's Sand Eel, Blanton's Whistler, Sanchez Double Bunny, Lefty's Deceiver, and poppers.

Bluefish

Notes: Perhaps the ocean's most voracious eaters, they usually jump and fight hard.
Water Types: River mouths, surf, and channels
Size: Average in the 5- to 12-pound range, seldom exceeding 20 pounds
Food Preferences: Herring, silversides, and other various bait fish

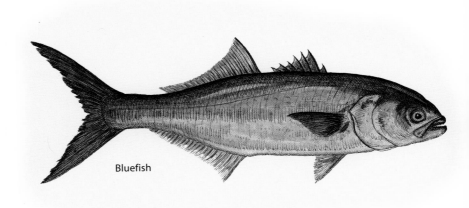

Bluefish

Blanton's Whistler Fly

Handling Concerns: Dangerously sharp teeth! Bluefish seem to have
   excellent vision out of the water and are known to give terrible
   bites. Hold the fish firmly and always remove the fly with pliers.

Recommended Tackle: (Based on a 10-pound bluefish)

   ROD: 9-foot for an 8-weight line

   REEL CAPACITY: 150–200 yards of 20-pound backing

   LINE: 8-weight floating—WF8F

   LEADER: Type C, 3- to 6-foot, 12-pound tippet, 40-pound wire shock tippet

   FLIES: The best hook sizes are 1/0 to 4/0 and although white works
   great, when blues are feeding anything works. Excellent patterns
   include the popper, Lefty's Deceiver, Blanton's Whistler, Tabory's
   Sand Eel, and Sanchez Double Bunny.

Red Drum (Channel Bass or Redfish)

Notes: The red drum is a determined fighter that frequently tails like a bonefish in shallow water and takes flies well.

Water Types: Grassy flats, mangrove shorelines, tidal creeks, and estuaries, as well as channels and deep river holes and shoreline pockets

Size: Average size is in the 5- to 10-pound range, can reach 60 pounds

Food Preferences: Mullet and other various bait fish, fry, shrimp, and crab

Handling Concerns: Beware of crushers in rear of the mouth that are used for crushing the shells of crustaceans and avoid sharp gill rakers.

Recommended Tackle: (Based on an 8-pound redfish)

ROD: 9-foot for an 8-weight line

REEL CAPACITY: 150–200 yards of 20-pound backing

LINE: 8-weight floating—WF8F

LEADER: Type A, 9-foot, 12-pound tippet

FLIES: The best hook sizes include 2 to 2/0 and favorite colors include brightly mixed combinations of red, orange, chartreuse, and white. Top patterns include the Lefty's Deceiver, Bend Back, Glass Minnow, Nix's Epoxy Fly, and small poppers.

Red Drum

Glass Minnow Fly

Spotted Sea Trout

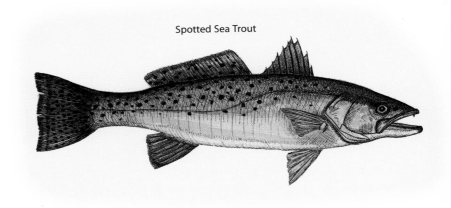

Clouser Deep Minnow Fly

Spotted Sea Trout

Notes: The spotted sea trout is one of the most popular game fish
  of the Gulf states. Often it is mistaken for weakfish.
Water Types: River mouths and bordering grassy flats
Size: Seldom larger than 8 pounds
Food Preferences: Shrimp, crab, and various bait fish
Handling Concerns: Avoid the canine-like teeth in large fish.
Recommended Tackle: (Based on a 5-pound sea trout)
  ROD: 9-foot for an 8-weight line
  REEL CAPACITY: 150–200 yards of 20-pound backing
  LINE: 8-weight floating—WF8F
  LEADER: Type A, 9-foot, 8-pound tippet
  FLIES: The best hook sizes are 4 to 2/0 and favorite colors include
  combinations of chartreuse, white, yellow, pink, green, red, and
  orange. Excellent patterns include the Clouser Deep Minnow,
  Lefty's Deceiver, Snapping Shrimp, poppers, and permit crab
  imitations.

Barracuda ("Cuda")

Notes: The pike of the ocean. These ferocious fish swarm the world's warm oceans in search of their prey. They take flies well (especially poppers) and are fantastic fly rod game fish.

Water Types: All six types. Flats and channels are the best place to fish for them.

Size: Barracuda come in a wide variety of sizes, from 2 to over 60 pounds.

Food Preferences: Needlefish, mullet, and other bait fish as well as any injured or exhausted game fish, such as bonefish and smaller barracuda

Handling Concerns: Barracuda have razor-sharp teeth and can be extremely dangerous. Cautiously use long nosed pliers for fly removal.

Barracuda

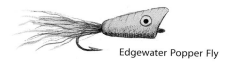

Edgewater Popper Fly

Recommended Tackle: (Based on a 10- to 20-pound barracuda)

ROD: 9-foot for a 10-weight line

REEL CAPACITY: These fish make long runs at lightning speeds. A good drag is important and the reel should hold 200–300 yards of 20- to 30-pound backing.

LINE: 10-weight floating—WF10F

LEADER: Type C, 6- to 9-foot, 15-pound tippet, 40-pound wire shock tippet

FLIES: The best hook sizes range from 2/0 to 5/0 and favorite colors are white, orange, chartreuse, and red. Excellent patterns include a variety of poppers, Dahlberg Diver, Braided Needle Fish, Lefty's Deceiver, and the Tarpon Glo.

Blacktip Shark

Notes: "Sharks on a fly rod!" exclaim most beginning saltwater fly anglers. Yes, sharks are excellent fly rod quarry. There are many species such as the blacktip, lemon, sand, and bull sharks, just to name a few, that are all great fun on flies.

Water Types: All six types. Flats and channels are the best places to fly fish for them.

Size: Sharks come in all sizes from 2 to 15 feet. 2- to 6-footers that cruise the flats provide the best fly rod action. I cast to any shark I see; the largest I have ever brought to the boat was a bull shark that was 7 feet long and probably over 200 pounds. That fish took a 2\0 boilermaker popper—not a bad fish for a dry fly.

Food Preferences: Any bait fish or injured game fish

Handling Concerns: Sharks have abrasive skin—much like sand paper—and sharp teeth. Always use pliers for fly removal. Also beware that they have cartilage rather than bones and have been known to bite a hand that seems out of reach. Hold a shark tightly right behind the head to avoid being bitten. Never take a large shark on board. Instead, release it by cutting the leader and forfeiting the fly to the shark.

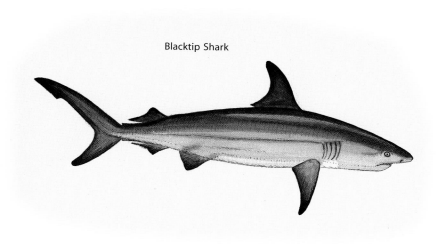

Blacktip Shark

Pencil Popper Fly

Recommended Tackle: (Based on a 3-foot blacktip shark)

ROD: 9-foot for a 8-weight line

REEL CAPACITY: A reel with a good drag and 150–200 yards of 20-pound backing will do the job.

LINE: 8-weight floating—WF8F

LEADER: Type C, 3- to 6-foot, 15-pound tippet, 40-pound wire shock tippet

Flies: The best hook sizes range from 2/0 to 4/0 and any bright colors work best. Excellent patterns include the Pencil Popper, Dahlberg Diver, Lefty's Deceiver, Tarpon Glo, and Blanton's Whistler.

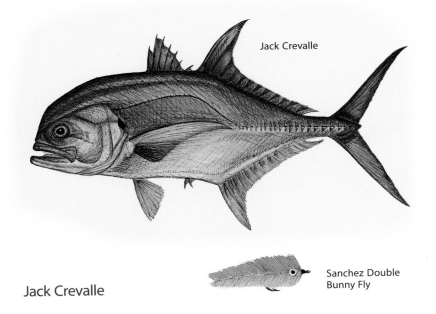

Jack Crevalle

Sanchez Double
Bunny Fly

Jack Crevalle

Notes: Just one of many jack family members. These fierce hunters often roam in schools herding and crashing schools of bait fish. They have amazing strength and speed and will easily tire an angler.

Water Types: Found in all six types of water.

Size: The jack crevalle averages 8 to 12 pounds, but occasionally exceeds 40 pounds. The giant trevally, commonly sought in the Pacific Ocean, is the largest member of the jack family, exceeding 100 pounds.

Food Preferences: Any bait fish or injured game fish, shrimp, and crab

Handling Concerns: Watch for sharp spines on the rear of the belly, and an abrasive tail.

Recommended Tackle: (Based on a 10-pound jack crevalle)

ROD: 9-foot for an 8-weight line

REEL CAPACITY: 150–200 yards of 20-pound backing

LINES: 8-weight floating—WF8F or 8-weight intermediate sinking—WF8I

LEADER: Type B, 6- to 9-foot, 15-pound tippet, 50-pound mono shock tippet

FLIES: The best hook sizes are 2/0 and 3/0 and a variety of colors will work. Excellent patterns include the popper, Dahlberg Diver, Lefty's Deceiver, Sanchez Double Bunny, and Blanton's Whistler.

Mutton Snapper

Notes: Snappers provide vicious strikes and stunningly powerful first runs. The mutton snapper is among the most commonly pursued snappers. It is easily distinguished from other snappers by its black spot near the tail. Other species include red, mangrove, dog, and cubera snappers, to name a few.

Water Types: Flats, river mouths, channels, and coral reefs

Size: Most fly-rod-size snappers run 5 to 15 pounds, but some species can exceed 60 pounds.

Food Preferences: Various bait fish, shrimp, and crab

Handling Concerns: Because of its large, sharp teeth and enormously strong jaws, use extreme caution while unhooking a snapper. Pliers are necessary.

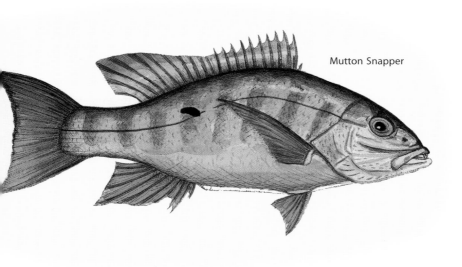

Mutton Snapper

Lefty's Deceiver

Recommended tackle: (Based on a 8- to 12-pound mutton snapper)

ROD: 9-foot for a 10-weight line

REEL CAPACITY: 150–200 yards of 20-pound backing. Long runs are unlikely, but you need a reel with a powerful drag to keep a snapper from returning to structure.

LINES: 10-weight floating—WF10F or 10-weight intermediate sinking—WF10I

LEADERS: Type B or C, 9-foot, 15-pound tippet, 40-pound mono or wire shock tippet

FLIES: The best hook sizes range from 2/0 to 4/0. Excellent patterns include the Lefty's Deceiver, Blanton's Whistler, Sanchez Double Bunny, Dahlberg Diver, and poppers.

Spanish Mackerel

Notes: Just one of many mackerel species. Because of the various water types in which they can be found, mackerel are often accidentally caught while seeking other game fish. They provide jolting strikes and fast runs.

Water Types: River mouths and estuaries, surf, reefs, and blue water

Size: Here are a few of the common species and their maximum sizes: chub mackerel, 2 pounds; Spanish mackerel, 15 pounds; king mackerel, 90 pounds; wahoo, 160 pounds. Any mackerel over 60 pounds would be an incredible feat landed on today's fly fishing tackle under IGFA regulations.

Food Preferences: Any bait fish

Handling Concerns: All mackerel have razor-sharp, scissor-like teeth. Cautiously use long nose pliers for fly removal.

Recommended Tackle: (Based on a 4-pound Spanish mackerel)

ROD: 9-feet for an 8-weight line

REEL CAPACITY: 150–200 yards of 20-pound backing

LINE: 8-weight floating—WF8F or 8-weight intermediate sinking—WF8I

LEADER: Type A, 9-foot, 8-pound tippet. Regardless of their sharp teeth, they are often too smart for shock tippets of any sort.

Flies: The best hook sizes range from 2 to 2/0 and bright colors mixed with white work well. Excellent patterns include the Clouser Deep Minnow, Lefty's Deceiver, Tabory's Sand Eel, Blanton's Whistler, Sanchez Double Bunny, and Bend Back.

Spanish Mackerel

Clouser Deep Minnow Fly

Bonito

Notes: The bonito is in the mackerel and tuna family. They are all well known for their smoking first runs that often exceed 100 yards.

Water Types: Just beyond shoreline casting range off river mouths and surf, as well as in blue water

Size: Average in the 3- to 6-pound range, rarely exceeding 8 pounds

Handling Concerns: Avoid the sharp teeth. Cautiously use long nose pliers for fly removal.

Recommended Tackle: (Based on a 4-pound bonito)
ROD: 9-foot for an 8-weight line

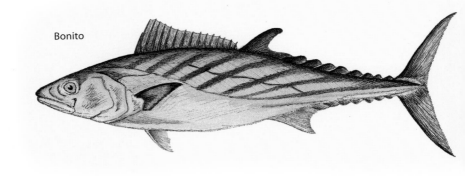

Bonito

Bend Back Fly

REEL CAPACITY: 150–200 yards of 20-pound backing
LINE: 8-weight intermediate sinking—WF8I
LEADER: Type A, 9-foot, 8-pound tippet. Regardless of their sharp teeth, they are often too smart for shock tippets of any sort.
FLIES: The best hook sizes range from 2 to 2/0 and favorite color and combinations should always include white. Excellent patterns include Lefty's Deceiver, Clouser Deep Minnow, Tabory's Sand Eel, Glass Minnow, and the Bend Back.

Blackfin Tuna

Notes: There are many species of tuna. Pound for pound they are one of the ocean's strongest fish.
Water Type: Blue water
Size: Here are some of the common species and their maximum sizes: blackfin, 50 pounds; skipjack, 80 pounds; longtail, 90 pounds; albacore, 100 pounds; dog tooth, 300 pounds; yellowfin, 400 pounds; big eye, 480 pounds; and bluefin, 1800 pounds. Specimens exceeding 100 pounds are nearly impossible to land on today's fly fishing equipment.

Food Preferences: Squid, octopus, shrimp, flying fish, herring, and other various bait fish, as well as smaller game fish such as mackerel

Handling Concerns: Tire a large tuna before bringing on board. Otherwise it's likely to smash you and your boat.

Recommended Tackle: (Based on a 12- to 15-pound blackfin tuna)

ROD: 9-feet for a 10-weight line

REEL CAPACITY: 300 yards of 30-pound backing

LINE: 10-weight sinking—WF10S

LEADER: Type B, 6-foot, 15-pound tippet, 60-pound mono shock tippet

FLIES: The best hook sizes are 1/0 to 4/0 and favorite colors are white, yellow, and green, in any combination. Excellent patterns include the Clouser Deep Minnow, Lefty's Deceiver, Blanton's Whistler, Sanchez Double Bunny, and poppers.

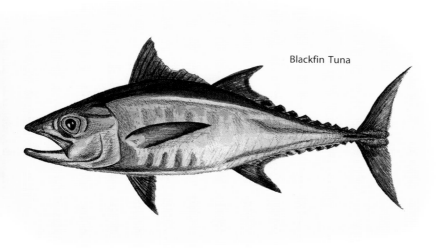

Blackfin Tuna

Blanton's Whistler Fly

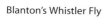

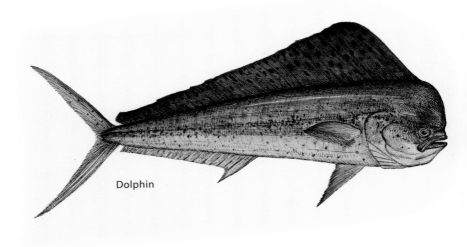

Dolphin

Sanchez Double Bunny Fly

Dolphin (Dorado or Mahimahi)

Notes: These brilliantly colored fish provide smashing strikes and acrobatic aerial battles. They are the most commonly sought after blue water species.

Water Type: Blue water

Size: Average size is about 8 to 15 pounds; large ones, called bulls, exceed 60 pounds.

Food Preferences: Squid, flying fish, herring, and other various bait fish, as well as smaller game fish such as mackerel

Handling Concerns: Fully exhaust a dolphin before boating it to avoid injury from violent thrashing.

Recommended Tackle: (Based on a 15-pound dolphin)

ROD: 9-foot for a 10-weight line

REEL CAPACITY: 200–300 yards of 20- to 30-pound backing.

LINE: 10-weight floating—WF10F

LEADER: Type B, 6- to 9-foot, 15-pound tippet, 60-pound mono shock tippet

FLIES: The best hook sizes range from 3/0 to 5/0 and favorite color combinations include white with bright colors. Excellent patterns include the popper, Lefty's Deceiver, Blanton's Whistler, Sanchez Double Bunny, and the Bend Back.

Billfish

Notes: There are several species of billfish and fly fishing for them was once considered an impossibility. Fly fishing for sailfish is now common and those who have caught sails seek marlin. Billfish are best known for their great acrobatic fighting power.

Water Type: Blue water

Size: Here are the species and their maximum sizes: spearfish, 100 pounds; Atlantic sailfish, 130 pounds; Pacific sailfish, 200 pounds; white marlin, 200 pounds; striped marlin, 500 pounds; black marlin, 1900 pounds; and blue marlin, over 2000 pounds. It is probably best not to attempt a billfish exceeding 200 pounds unless you are extremely experienced and in superb physical shape; even then don't expect to land it!

Food Preferences: Squid, octopus, various bait fish, and game fish such as mackerel and bonito, as well as small tuna and dolphin

Handling Concerns: Never bring a billfish on board until it is fully exhausted. Its strength alone can cause great harm to you and the fish. Beware of the bill.

Recommended Tackle: (Based on an 80-pound Pacific sailfish)

ROD: 8½- to 9-foot for a 12- to 14-weight line

REEL CAPACITY: 400 yards of 30-pound backing. *Special Note:* Billfish of over 100 pounds can exceed swimming speeds of over 65

Pacific Sailfish

Billfish Mullet Fly with Popper Head

miles per hour. I advise the use of mono running line between your backing and your fly line to add stretch to your system. This will act as a shock absorber during these amazing runs. Use 100 feet of 40-pound test. Use an Albright Knot to attach it to the backing and a Spider Hitch loop at the end that will attach to the fly line. As always, whip a loop in the end of your fly line and loop the two sections together.

LINE: Sinking Shooting taper—ST13S. A 30-foot shooting taper fly line is preferable to a standard 80- to 120-foot fly line. Less fly line means less drag through the water, and during the awesome run of a billfish, it is an advantage that can make the difference between landing and losing one of these great game fish.

LEADER: Type B, 9-foot, 20-pound tippet, 100-pound mono shock tippet

FLIES: The best hook sizes range from 3/0 to 5/0. If you are using a teaser, it is important that the color of your fly matches it. Use tandem hook flies, with the trailer either being turned up or off to one side. If you are fishing for a possible IGFA record then be sure that the eye of each hook is no farther apart than six inches, and that the second hook does not extend past the fly's wing material. Excellent patterns include Curcione's Big Game Fly, Fernandez's Big Fish Fly, Lefty's Deceiver, or the Billfish Mullet.

Poppers also work well for billfish. The noise made by a popper helps billfish to locate a fly after a teaser has been pulled from the water. All the flies described above can be made into a popper. Simply make a hole through an Ethafoam popper head so that you can slide it onto a shock tippet before you attach the fly. Put it on, and once the fly is attached, force it down to the head of the fly. It is a good idea to secure it with a drop of zap-a-gap glue so that during a battle it will not slide up the leader and entice a strike from another fish, likely ending in disaster. You have just made a custom popper.

Sailfish release.

Even the unusual jewfish will eat a fly.

In Conclusion

THE SEVENTEEN DIFFERENT SPECIES listed could keep any angler content for a long time, but remember that there are a lot more that can be taken on fly. Whether it's a glamorous blue water game fish such as a wahoo, or the interesting looking boxfish that darts about the flats, overshadowed by more popular game fish, each species deserves some attention. If you really want a challenge, try catching the numerous sheepshead that inhabit grassy flats and shallow bays, or for that matter, perhaps even a tailing parrot fish milling along the coral reef. Both of these fish add a new dimension to the term "spooky."

Always remember that regardless of where you visit or travel, if there is saltwater, then surely there is potential for saltwater fly fishing.

Grouper

TOP: Deflated Puffer. BOTTOM: Inflated Puffer.

TOP: **Bluefin Trevally.** BOTTOM: Boxfish.

SALTWATER EQUIPMENT CHECKLIST

THE FOLLOWING CHECKLIST represents the absolute minimum equipment that you should carry on a trip to the salt. You may want to add other items depending on your location and the specific demands of that location.

- [ ] Rods (Take more than one.)
- [ ] Reels (See page 40 on reel types.)
- [ ] Lines (Make sure you have at least one spare line for the fish that steals your entire outfit.)
- [ ] Backing (Take an extra spool just in case . . .)
- [ ] Leaders in the appropriate size and style (Include extra tippet material in the appropriate sizes and style; will you need shock tippets? Put 'em in.)
- [ ] Hook sharpener
- [ ] WD-40, reel oil, or some other anti-rust lubricant (double bag in case of leaks)
- [ ] Appropriate flies, and if you tie, extra hooks and materials in the correct sizes
- [ ] Appropriate footwear (flats booties in the tropics, waders in cooler climates)
- [ ] Vest, fanny pack, day pack, or some other suitable way to carry your gear
- [ ] Lightweight breathable hat (especially in warm climates)

☐ Warm, quick-drying hat (or rain hat)

☐ Rain Gear (even in the tropics)

☐ Long underwear (tops and bottoms) in northern climates

☐ Quick-drying long pants (Supplex is good.)

☐ Quick-drying shirts—in warm climates, wear light, reflective colors

☐ Shorts

☐ Sun screen—use it frequently

☐ Polarized sunglasses

☐ Line clippers (Cheap toenail clippers from any drugstore work fine. They eventually rust out, but will last a few weeks.)

☐ Stripping basket

☐ Flashlight

☐ Insect repellent

☐ First aid kit—include an antifungal foot ointment and, if you'll be in boats on rough water, some kind of antiseasickness medication, and any prescription medications that you need.

☐ Pliers or universal tool (e.g. Leatherman)—Keep these liberally doused in oil to retard rust. Also, a stainless steel tool will resist rust better.

☐ Water bottle (and in some locations, purification tablets)

☐ Heavy-duty gloves for fish with abrasive skin

☐ Passport (if you go anywhere outside the U.S.)

And last, but not least,

☐ *Currier's Quick and Easy Guide to Saltwater Fly Fishing!*

JEFF'S FLY BOX

WITH FLY PHOTOS BY DOUG O'LOONEY

WHEN I BEGAN TO FLY FISH the salt, there were only a handful of patterns specifically designed for the salt. With these few patterns, and some concoctions of my own, I could fool most of the popular saltwater species.

Today the list of saltwater patterns has grown immensely. For example, just within the category of shrimp and crab patterns, there are hundreds of choices. Most of these patterns are excellent, but for the novice saltwater angler, the variety can be overwhelming.

Following is a list of fly patterns, including the colors and sizes of each that I carry in my saltwater fly box at all times. These are common patterns, available at most fly shops, or, if you tie flies, easy to tie. If you start with this selection of proven patterns as a base, you can fine tune your flies with other patterns that address specific situations.

Shrimp

Crazy Charlie—sizes 8 through 2 in white, tan, pink, green, and yellow
Snapping Shrimp—sizes 6 through 4
Nix's Epoxy Fly—sizes 6 through 4 in pink and root beer

Crab

McCrab—sizes 8 through 1/0
Del's Merkin Crab—sizes 6 through 1/0
Yarn Crab—sizes 8 through 1/0 in tan, olive, lime, or any combination of these colors

Streamers

Lefty's Deceiver—sizes 2 through 4/0 in blue/white, green/white, red/white, and green/yellow

Clouser Deep Minnow—sizes 8 through 1/0 in chartreuse/white, red/white, blue/white, and brown/beige

Blanton's Whistler—sizes 2/0 through 4/0 in red/yellow, orange/yellow, and red/white

Glass Minnow—sizes 4 through 1/0

Cockroach—sizes 2/0 through 4/0

Tarpon Glo—sizes 2/0 through 4/0

Bend Back—sizes 2 through 2/0

Sanchez Double Bunny—sizes 2/0 through 4/0 in blue/white and green/white

Braided Needle Fish—size 2/0 in orange or chartreuse

Tabory's Sand Eel—sizes 4 through 1/0

Sanchez Squid—sizes 2/0 through 6/0

Poppers

Dahlberg Diver—sizes 2 through 4/0 in white, black, orange, and chartreuse

Edgewater Popper—sizes 2 through 3/0 in white, yellow, chartreuse, and blue

Pencil Popper—sizes 2 through 2/0 in white, yellow, chartreuse, and blue

Bend Back

Blanton's Whistler

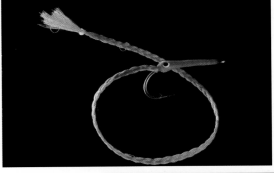

Braided Needle Fish

Clouser Deep Minnow

Cockroach

Crazy Charlie

Dahlberg Diver

Del's Merkin Crab

Edgewater Popper

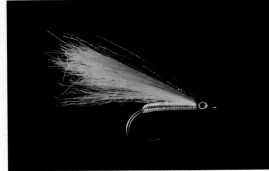

Glass Minnow

Lefty's Deceiver

McCrab

Nix's Epoxy Fly

Pencil Popper

Sanchez Double Bunny

Sanchez Squid

Snapping Shrimp

Tabory's Sand Eel

Tarpon Glo

Yarn Crab

Appendix C

JEFF'S TIPS FOR SALTWATER SUCCESS

BY NOW YOU HAVE COMPLETED the majority of *Currier's Quick and Easy Guide to Saltwater Fly Fishing*. You are armed with a fundamental knowledge to meet the final fly fishing frontier: saltwater. You will enjoy it.

It is important to understand that this book doesn't present everything there is to know about saltwater fly fishing. For instance, there are many alternative knots, some stronger, some weaker, or equal in strength but more difficult to tie. The selections I've included are designed for easy understanding. Techniques discussed will be easier to master once you've applied them.

If you begin with this book and take a love for the salt as I have, you will want to learn more. I highly recommend Lefty Kreh's *Fly Fishing in Salt Water*, as well as Lou Tabory's *Inshore Fly Fishing*. These two books provide extensive information on the sport and include nearly all the other knots and techniques not addressed here. Lefty and Lou are two of many expert instructors on saltwater fly fishing you will encounter. See the bibliography for other helpful references on fly fishing the salt.

But, as with any pursuit, there are a number of simple techniques, habits, and rules that will enhance your saltwater experience. Follow these tips faithfully and you will have more success (and, consequently, more fun) on the salt.

Tips for Saltwater Fly Fishing

1. Saltwater corrodes valuable fishing equipment. Thoroughly clean it all after each outing. Reels will occasionally need additional oiling. Penn Reel oil works as well as anything.

2. Routinely check your knots, both new and old. A fish should never be lost because of a poor knot.

3. Never fish a fly without a razor sharp hook. A small bastard file obtainable from hardware or saltwater tackle stores works as an excellent sharpener. The best procedure is to hold the fly with your pliers and file the hook point in a triangular fashion. A sharp hook will stick to your fingernail.

4. Always be prepared to cast your best. Distance, speed, and accuracy are essential. Learn the Double Haul. *Practice your casting before you go.*

5. Extra line always seems to tangle around your feet when you're standing on the deck of a boat. Take off your shoes and socks (put sun screen on the tops of your feet). You'll feel the coils of extra line with your toes and stay off them.

6. Never pull a fly away from a feeding fish. It is common to set the hook on a fish charging the fly before he actually takes it. It's like buck fever. If you don't feel him, don't set the hook.

7. When sight fishing from a boat, use the clock system to describe fish location. The bow points to 12 o'clock and you know the rest. Example: "Bonefish at 2 o'clock! Cast fifty feet!" When you have trouble seeing the target, point your rod tip and let your guide or friend adjust your view to the target.

8. When you see predators (bluefish, stripers, etc.) herding and busting bait fish at the surface, don't drive the boat right up to the frenzy. You'll spook the school. That mass of churning bait slowly moves "upcurrent." Circle it, cut the boat engine and drift into place ahead of it. Let the action come towards you.

9. It's frustrating when bluefish and stripers are slashing on the surface at a ball of bait fish so thick that your fly is lost in the mass. Cast and slap your line down hard. The bait fish panic and move to the

sides, leaving a clean V of water in the middle for your fly or popper to pass through.

10. Consider turning your reel handle with your most dexterous hand for saltwater fly fishing and especially in blue water. Extra strength in this hand may help you endure a long battle with a larger fish.

11. The suction of rays swimming along the bottom often stirs up crab and shrimp. Always place a cast just behind them in the hope of picking up a following feeding game fish.

12. If you plan to purchase new rods for saltwater, invest in multiple-piece travel rods. Today, the quality of these rods is equal to two-piece rods. Some of the best saltwater destinations require flight travel and I feel better if my rods are carry-on items.

13. Any trip near saltwater whether it be a honeymoon, anniversary, vacation, or business, is a good excuse to involve a fly rod. Don't leave home without one!

Map Key
LOCATIONS OF SPECIES

Bonefish—B
Permit—P
Tarpon—T
Snook—S
Striped Bass—SB
Bluefish—BL
Red Drum—R
Sea Trout—ST
Barracuda—C
Black Tip Shark and other members of the shark family—SH
Jack Crevalle and other members of the Jack family—J
Mutton Snapper—SN
Bonito—BO
Dolphin—D
Tuna—TU
Sailfish—SF

CAPITALIZED—Species is commonly found
small letters—Species is occasionally found
Red—Seasonal April–September
Blue—Seasonal October–March

SALTWATER FISH DISTRIBUTION
USA

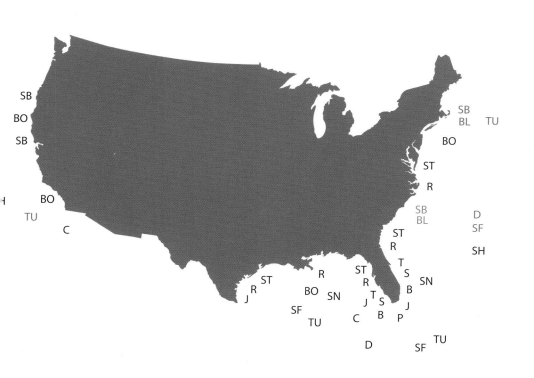

SALTWATER FISH DISTRIBUTION
THE WORLD

See map key on page 110.

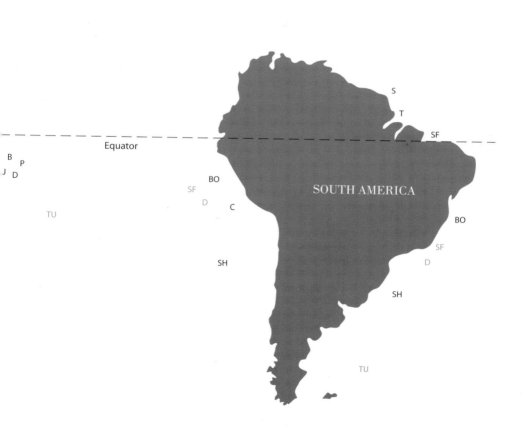

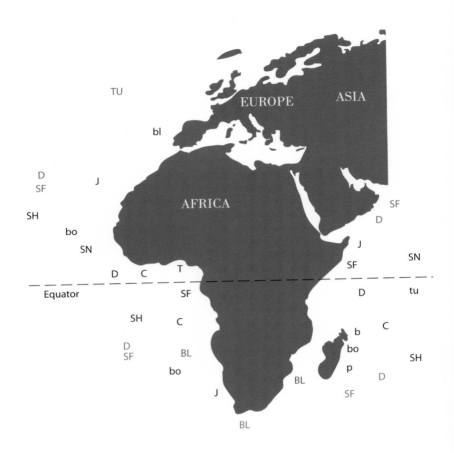

See map key on page 110.

See map key on page 110.

Most anglers who have fished flats bordering a reef have cast, usually unsuccessfully, to parrot fish, but years of persistence finally paid off when this parrot struck my Crazy Charlie.

BIBLIOGRAPHY

HERE IS A LIST OF BOOKS that can provide you with more information. These are books that I often use myself to learn more about all aspects of saltwater fishing.

Babson, Stanley M. *Bonefishing*. New York: Winchester, 1973.

Brown, Dick. *Fly Fishing for Bonefish*. New York: Lyons & Burford, Publishers, 1993.

Burchett, Michael, Marc Dando and Geoffrey Waller. *Sealife*. Washington, D.C.: Smithsonian Institution Press, 1996.

Cole, John. *Tarpon Quest*. New York: Lyons & Burford, Publishers, 1991.

Combs, Trey. *Bluewater Fly Fishing*. New York: Lyons & Burford, Publishers, 1996.

Curcione, Nick. *The Orvis Guide to Saltwater Fly Fishing*. Harrisburg, Pa.: Stackpole Books, 1994.

Goadby, Peter. *Saltwater Gamefishing*. Camden, Maine: International Marine Publishing, 1992.

Karas, Nick. *The Striped Bass*. New York: Lyons & Burford, Publishers, 1993.

Kaufmann, Randall. *Fly Patterns of Umpqua Feather Merchants*. Glide, Oreg.: Umpqua Feather Merchants, 1995.

_____. *Bonefishing with a Fly*. Portland, Oreg.: Western Fisherman's Press, 1992.

Kreh, Lefty. *Fly Fishing in Salt Water*. New York: Lyons & Burford, Publishers, 1987.

_____. *Salt Water Fly Patterns*. Fullerton, Calif.: Maral, Inc., [1980–1989].

McClane, A. J. *McClane's Field Guide to Saltwater Fishes of North America*. New York: Holt, Rinehart, and Winston, 1978.

_____, ed. *McClane's New Standard Fishing Encyclopedia*. New York: Holt, Rinehart, and Winston, 1974.

Robins, C. Richard, et al. *A Field Guide to Atlantic Coast Fishes of North America*. Peterson Field Guide Series, No. 32. New York: Houghton Mifflin, 1986.

Rogers, Neal and Linda. *Saltwater Fly Fishing Magic*. New York: Lyons & Burford, Publishers, 1993.

Samson, Jack. *Saltwater Fly Fishing*. Harrisburg, Pa.: Stackpole Books, 1991.

Sargent, Frank. *The Redfish Book*. Lakeland, Fla.: Larsen's Outdoor Publishing, 1991.

_____. *The Snook Book*. Lakeland, Fla.: Larsen's Outdoor Publishing, 1990.

_____. *The Tarpon Book*. Lakeland, Fla.: Larsen's Outdoor Publishing, 1991.

Sosin, Mark. *Practical Saltwater Fly Fishing*. New York: Lyons & Burford, Publishers, 1989.

Sosin, Mark and Lefty Kreh. *Fishing the Flats*. New York: Lyons & Burford, Publishers, 1983.

_____. *Practical Fishing Knots II*. New York: Lyons & Burford, Publishers, 1991.

Stewart, Dick and Farrow Allen. *Flies for Saltwater*. North Conway, N.H.: Mountain Pond Publishing, 1992.

Tabory, Lou. *Lou Tabory's Guide to Saltwater Baits and Their Imitations*. New York: Lyons & Burford, Publishers, 1995.

_____. *Inshore Fly Fishing*. New York: Lyons & Burford, Publishers, 1992.

INDEX